My Roller Coaster Ride

A true story of a trader's struggle
Most investment books don't cover
What investors need to know

Beth Fiedler

Copyright © 2014 Beth Fiedler

ISBN: 978-0-9920937-5-4

All rights reserved. No part of this book may be reproduced or transmitted in any form or by any means, electronic or mechanical, including photocopying, recording, or by any information storage and retrieval system, without permission in writing from the copyright owner.

This book is presented solely for educational purposes. The author and publisher are in no way liable for any misuse of the material. It is sold with the understanding that the author and publisher are not engaged in rendering legal, accounting or financial advisory services. If legal or other expert assistance is required, the services of a competent professional should be sought.

The material in this book may include information, products or services by third parties. Third Party materials comprise of the products and opinions expressed by their owners. As such, the author and publisher of this book do not assume responsibility or liability of any Third Party materials or opinions.

Although the author and publisher have made every effort to ensure that the information in this book was correct at press time, the author and publisher do not assume and hereby disclaim any liability to any party for any loss, damage, or disruption caused by errors or omissions, whether such errors or omissions result from negligence, accident, or any other cause. References are provided for informational purposes only and do not constitute endorsement of any websites or other sources. Readers should be aware that the websites listed in this book may change.

This book was printed in the United States of America.

DEDICATION

Dedicated to You

It is a great step to take!

It is going to be fruitful and enjoy your learning!

ACKNOWLEDGMENTS

With the deepest gratitude I would like to thank my husband Nelson, who has been extremely supportive since I started my Futures learning. It was the most challenging journey I have ever taken.

I was very fortunate to have Nelson standing by me all the time. His confidence in me was the motivating force behind my learning success. There were uncountable moments I was very close to mental or physical collapses. With his care, I was able to recover and continued my pursuit. His encouragement has been my inspiration to write this book.

I would also like to thank my elder sister Eva who has always been there for me regardless of our geographical locations. It is a comfortable feeling to know that she is out there for me.

Terry, a very dear friend who has known me for decades, I appreciate very much her love and support. She is always there showering me with compliments and smiles.

For my trading friends: Ann, Alan, Baruch, Ben, Big Mike, Birgir, Bluemele, Cory, David The Wizard, Eddie, Eric J, Jeff C, Harry Fat Tails, Hugo, Jungian, Kirk The Captain, MetalTrade, Mike W, Monpere, Perry, Rob, Roger, Steve plus many others from different parts of the world, they have been very generous in sharing their knowledge and experience with me. Thank you!

For my trading platform partner NinjaTrader, I am grateful for the partnership opportunity and support I have been receiving from their team members especially Ray, Ryan M and Ryan S.

CONTENTS

INTRODUCTION

FOREWORD 1

WHO AM I? 3

A NEW LEAF 4

INITIAL ENCOUNTER

MY EXPERIENCE IN ADVISORY SERVICES 5

AN EVENTFUL TRADING WEEK 9

NEXT MOVE

WHAT MAKES FUTURES TRADING APPEALING? ... 13

HOW I STARTED MY FUTURES LEARNING? 14

MY SELF-LEARNING JOURNEY 17

TRADING ROOM EXPERIENCE 22

EXPECTATION VERSUS REALITY

WHAT TO EXPECT? 33

BLACK HOLE 36

TIME WARP 39

JUSTIFY EVERY MOVE? 41

SYSTEM (SOUL) SEARCH 43

WHAT DID I WANT? 45

SAME TRADING SYSTEM GENERATES DIFFERENT TRADING RESULTS?	48

BREAKTHROUGH

TRADING IS A BUSINESS	51
IT IS A MIND GAME	54
DO WE HAVE A MATCH?	58
PERFECT MATCH	61
TURNED INTO A MECHANICAL TRADER	63
SUPPORT AND RESISTANCE (S/R)	66
TRADITIONAL/DISCRETIONARY OR AUTOMATED TRADING?	68
HOW TO BECOME A CONSISTENTLY SUCCESSFUL TRADER?	71
THE HOLY GRAIL	74

ACTION PLAN

MARKET REPLAY VS SIMULATION VS LIVE TRADING	75
MY FAVORITE TRADING SYSTEMS	78
FAVORITE SIGNAL	80
STRATEGY ANALYZER	83
TRADING PLAN	85
DAILY GAME PLAN	89

S.M.A.R.T. – REALITY CHECK	91
REVIEW AND REFLECTION (R&R)	94
HOW TO VALIDATE A SYSTEM'S PERFORMANCE?	97
HOW TO TABULATE EXPECTANCY?	101
HOW TO GROW AN ACCOUNT?	103
ON YOUR MARK, GET SET, BEFORE GO	108

THE WINNING STRATEGY

WANT WHAT THE MARKET WANTS	109
K.I.S.S.	112
WHEN NOT TO TRADE	114
QUITTING IS A TRADING DECISION	116
CONTINUED LEARNING AND RESEARCH	119
COMMON TRADING MISTAKES	121

FINANCIAL PLANNING

UNDERSTAND MY FINANCES	129
PREPARE A DRAFT INVESTMENT PLAN	132
MAKE A PLAN	134
KEEPING TRACK	138
NO TRADING IF	140
INVESTMENT – FRAME OF MIND	141
AN IMPORTANT MOVE	143

MAKE AN INFORMED DECISION

WHAT WOULD I DO DIFFERENTLY? 145

TO-DO LIST 150

CHECKLIST 154

ALERT! 158

CALL FOR ACTION 161

ENDING NOTE

LOSSES AND GAINS 163

CONCLUSION 165

MY VISION 167

BEFORE AND AFTER 169

SIGN-UP 171

BONUS ARTICLES 172

LEGEND 177

BIOGRAPHY 178

INTRODUCTION

FOREWORD

Between 2009 and 2011, I spent close to 20,000 hours on Futures self-learning. I ended up designing a trading system and leased it to those who would like to learn more about Futures trading. In 2013, The Fiedler's were on the Dragons' Den pitching an educational proposal to the dragons. Unfortunately, most of the dragons knew nothing about Futures and we did not get an offer.

Upon our return, I tried to figure out what can I do to share my story so that others do not need to go through the same growing pains. I believe there must be more economical and easier ways to learn about trading without spending years and losing thousands of dollars.

I know there are thousands of investment and trading books out there. For example, different schools of thought on technical and fundamental analysis of the market. There are hundreds of trading systems and thousands of indicators out there claiming their services and products are safe havens for those who want to trade profitably.

I started writing this book - my attempt to share my experiences that are not yet covered out there. Who is my target audience? What value will my book bring to the readers?

My book is for those who have an open mind and would appreciate sharing a trader's real-life story. My Futures self-learning was not perfect. I repeatedly made the same mistakes. I was like thousands of traders out there trying to find a holy grail.

I failed uncountable times. I cried. I swore. I called myself "loser". I gathered my courage and started all over again.

I believe I have made most, if not all the trading and learning mistakes that anyone can and will make. Why am I exposing myself to the world? I want others to learn from my mistakes and do not repeat what I did!

This book is written in a simple language for most to understand. I hope this book will persuade the readers to start their learning with a correct attitude and expectation.

This book does not cover sophisticated analytical tools or systems or terminologies on trading. This book will not help the readers make money. This book is about not losing money and it is not about trading systems or profitable investment.

Readers will realize substantial time and resource savings after reading this book. To those who are serious about trading, I would like to urge them to go through the suggested checklist and commit to an action plan. An action plan must have specific timelines to accomplish all the recommended items.

I am confident that this book will shed light to those who have been sitting on the fence about Futures trading. This book will save time, pains and resources. It will give the readers a good idea on how to avoid the most common trading mistakes. It will shorten the readers' learning path. They will be in a better position to make a sensible trading decision.

Readers are welcome to sign-up for free access to the Tips Sheet I posted on-line. Please read the Sign-Up chapter for more details.

WHO AM I?

I am one of the millions around the world who want to become a profitable trader. I could be one of the most hardworking learners who spent days and nights learning and dreaming how to trade Futures profitably.

Most of us work 35-40 hours a week. I spent an average person's 8-10 years working life on learning how to trade Futures. Hundreds of friends asked me the following questions:

> Will you start your self-learning venture if you knew you would spend thousands of hours on it?

> What are the tangible rewards you have made from your Futures learning?

The cost associated with my self-learning venture was over US$200,000 (based on a minimum hourly pay of US$10/hour x 20,000 hours) exclusive of the resources and money I spent on programs, books and subscription.

The readers will get my answers from the book!

A NEW LEAF

I was born in Hong Kong and emigrated to Toronto on my own. I got married and relocated to Cambridge, Ontario.

We were living in an Eco zone with the Little Lake right in front of our beautiful home. Life was peaceful. Unfortunately, there were no job opportunities for me. Hundreds of applications were sent and no phone calls or emails suggesting an interview. Time passed by and I started looking for other alternatives.

I thought "Go natural and organic is the trend". I was able to source out some organic products at reasonable prices. Knocked on hundreds of doors for consignment and partnership. As a nobody, you can guess what happened. We kept the products for two years and donated them to shelters. That's how we turned lemons into lemonade for those who would appreciate our sharing.

What's next? I have experience in trading directional options and stocks based on paid advisory services. I did not make a fortune yet I enjoyed reasonable returns on investment before the crash in 2008.

I said to myself: "Let me try to make a living out of trading different financial instruments." I subscribed to multiple advisory services on directional options, option spreads and stocks.

INITIAL ENCOUNTER

MY EXPERIENCE IN ADVISORY SERVICES

Directional Options

I tried about 10 vendors within the first six months. Most were very affordable at a monthly US$50-$100 subscription. A few were free.

Then I started with a US$99 subscription with a big name and within weeks I was lured into their advisory services with a 4-digit price tag. The first few picks were winners and I made at least a 20% profit within hours or days.

Being a stay-at-home domestic engineer did turn me desperate and vulnerable. I ended up with an almost US$10,000 service plan with a directional options advisory company. I added a guaranteed profit-making term to protect my interest before making the first payment of a few thousand dollars. I was smart, right?

Wrong!!

I never got a chance to talk with a financial advisor directly. It was always an associate calling me with an option pick, namely a trading symbol and entry price. She told me, "Leave the trade open and wait for me to call again with exit instructions".

Beth Fiedler

When the suggested option picks all turned from profitable trades to losing ones, I went wild and kept pressing the associate to ask the advisor if I should exit with less damage. Her answer had always been "hold on to the trades and we still had time before the options expired".

I lost thousands on those outstanding options trades and some were 100% write-offs. Within months after subscribing to that options advisory company, I lost close to US$10,000 (not counting the thousands I paid for their subscription).

Confession: I did not really understand the risks associated with directional options.

Advice: Always keep a clear head and do not lose your "cool"! When it sounds too easy making money, stay away from it! It is a must to understand a financial instrument and its risks before making a move!

Stocks

I traded stocks based on paid advisory services and occasionally picks from friends (hearsay). My stocks had an original book value of $100,000. I held on to most of them based on the advisor's recommendation. Guess the current market value of these stocks? They account for less than 5% and simply not worth selling as I would pay more commission for their exit.

Confession: Picks from the advisor were hearsay too as I seldom did any research on the stocks before buying them. No stop order to protect my principal was a very bad practice!

Advice: Always have an exit plan for every stock purchase inclusive of profit-taking.

Option Spreads

After my directional options and stocks experience, I decided to learn how to trade option spreads. I paid over US$2,000 for an online option spreads program that came with a lifetime membership and free access to a trading room. With mentors hosting live webinars and active participation in a trading room with real-time market tips, I thought I would learn and make some profitable trades on a regular basis.

When we were in a trade, most of us did not cut our losses when it was time to exit based on predetermined rules. When we called and emailed our mentor, he often asked us to hold on to a losing trade. He said the market could not go further (up or down) and our trade would reverse to our favor.

Some fellow traders started adding more contracts for a better cost average. Within days, a 20% losing trade fell another 25%, then 50% and 75%. I exited most of my trades with less than 25% principal back to my account. Another US$5,000 down the drains!

Confession: Reality stroke again. Pride often obstructed my head and heart.

Advice: Always have an exit plan! Act on an exit plan diligently!

What happened to my lifetime membership and free access to a trading room?

Our mentors left the company and started their own business. The vendor closed the trading room and we lost our access to the membership website. I emailed and talked with the owner who runs the company. He made several promises to activate our membership and never did.

By the end of 2009, I asked myself very often "what did I do wrong?". I was with paid advisory vendors most of the time. How could I possibly lose so much? Over US$50,000 shrink less than a year was a huge blow to most? What's wrong with me? Did I lose my senses?

I did not cover every single detail in the My Experience In Advisory Services chapter. However, the following stood out loud and clear:

Paid advisory service is not the answer to a profitable investment! Investors are! Investors should always be responsible for every single investment and trading decision they make! Learn to become an informed investor!

I would share my Futures trading room experience in a separate chapter. I tried almost 10 trading rooms and over half of them were paid ones.

AN EVENTFUL TRADING WEEK

After realizing I can only count on myself to become successful in trading, I was very enthusiastic and diligent in doing research on the Internet. I became more receptive to free resources as my investment pool has shrunk substantially. I signed up for multiple community forums (for example, FOREX, Futures, options and stocks) and subscribed to over 20 newsletters.

I read thousands of posts, hundreds of threads and over 50 trading books; watched hundreds of videos; tried hundreds of indicators; experimented with over 100 trading systems inclusive of automated strategies; and tested out close to 10 trading platforms.

For the first few months, everyone could tell I was scattered everywhere because I was under the wrong perception that diversity was a key success factor. When I was extremely exhausted and ran out of both time and resources, I decided to focus on one community forum, one financial market (Futures) and one trading platform (NinjaTrader).

Based on my experience, NinjaTrader has always been the most user-friendly and readily available for both inexperienced and seasoned trading professionals. I was constantly in touch with their support team to familiarize myself with the platform's features and strategy development. I would like to emphasize the most effective way to learn is by doing and asking questions.

Number one (1) is your best friend! Focus on one trading system, one trading platform and one financial market (also one financial instrument). I was definitely not a good example. I often stretched myself too thin and was very aggressive until I learned how to become a disciplined trader. If the readers learn from my mistakes, they will be on a fast track to become a disciplined trader!

I spent hundreds of hours on learning, research and testing of trading systems. I started sim-trading two systems in January 2010. I did amazingly well and all trading mornings were profitable.

Tell me if the following plan looks good for an inexperienced Futures trader:

No of Instruments: 2
No of Trading Systems: 2 (a trending system and a scalping one)
No of Charts: 8
No of Trades: 3-5/morning
Trade Size: 2- to 3-contract trades

It was my daily game plan for the first two weeks in January 2010. With a plan to go live in February, I modified my game plan again in mid January as follows:

No of Instruments: 1 (from 2)
No of Trading Systems: 2 (unchanged)
No of Charts: 4 (from 8)
No of Trades: 3-5/morning (unchanged)
Trade Size: 2- to 3-contract trades (unchanged)

When my sim-trade account accumulated over US$1,000 profits in just one week in end January, I thought I was ready to go live in February and I did.

The first two trading mornings were profitable, ie 11 and 19 ticks at US$5/tick respectively. I got very excited. On the third morning, I started having lapses on my predetermined trading rules. It was a losing day of one tick (US$5) after three trades. On the fourth morning, I pulled up 8 charts and traded two Futures instruments.

Bear in mind that I never planned that way. It was a losing day of over US$100.

I had two losing days in a row and lost all the ticks I made for the first two mornings. I was not happy yet I was still hopeful that I would do well and regain my ticks on Friday.

What happened to the fifth trading morning of the first live trading week?

I was back with one Futures instrument. The first trade was a 3-tick winner (US$15). The second trade was a 42-tick loser (-US$210). After losing almost US$250 within minutes, I did not stop and continue with a third trade.

The third and last trade was a 2-contract trade and over 80 ticks in red! When the trade was not going in my direction, I added a second contract for a better average cost. The trading systems did not tell me to add and I had been ignoring all the entry rules for the last trade.

I froze when the trade went further down and I held on to it for over three hours before closing my position. No words could express the anxiety and stress I encountered.

I closed my trade because it was a Friday and my account did not have the required funds to hold the contracts over the weekend. It would be a disaster if my account was fully-funded. Instead of losing US$400 for the last trade, it could be thousands.

In one trading day, I lost almost US$700. I could not recall exactly what happened. I was shocked at my irrational trading behavior. I made a pledge to myself that until I found out how to become a disciplined trader and become one, I would not be trading my live account again.

Beth Fiedler

That eventful trading week was a life-changing event for me. I created my first trading thread and became a serious learner dedicating all my time and efforts on Futures learning.

NEXT MOVE

WHAT MAKES FUTURES TRADING APPEALING?

I am an active subscriber to over 20 trading vendors. Their daily emails always have an eye-catchy headlines such as

- 20-50 ticks per day in just one trade
- Absolutely nothing to purchase
- Add an extra income of $200-$300 daily
- Enjoy a lifestyle of your choice
- Enjoy financial freedom at your fingertips
- Try a failure-proof strategy free

No wonder most would think they could get rich fast and easy with Futures trading! Based on my experience, trading success can only be earned with commitment, hard work and a solid discipline.

We must have a good understanding on what we need to become successful. Please go through the FINANCIAL PLANNING and MAKE AN INFORMED DECISION sections.

Note: There is no shortcut to get rich fast and easy!

HOW I STARTED MY FUTURES LEARNING?

It was not intentional. I subscribed to an on-line option spread program. The program came with a trading room. The moderator occasionally called out some Futures signals. I could not resist taking one in May (my first Futures trade). The trade was profitable and I made US$50 within minutes.

I got connected with a few trading friends who recommended a breakout system. As an inexperienced Futures trader, I relied mostly on word-of-mouth. I bought a few trading books on the suggested breakout system and started my Futures learning.

I completed my readings within days and felt motivated to trade live. I subscribed to a trading room with a moderator calling out signals. Three of us (myself and two trading friends) thought we did our due diligence and were on our way to a profitable Futures career. I cover my trading room experience in a separate chapter.

Having tried almost 10 trading rooms, I will only recommend joining a trading room whose system meets our preference. For example, do we like breakout trades? How about reversal trades? There are false breakout trades too. Or a naked chart to focus on price movement only? Feel more protected with multiple indicators and charts?

It is like opening a can of worms and most will feel lost at the beginning. I did not spend too much time on technical and fundamental analysis tools. My learning started after my eventful trading week (which was on a separate chapter) and bad experience with paid advisors.

I did extensive research on trading systems and subscribed to multiple trading forums. Read thousands of posts on others' trading experience and started trying out hundreds of indicators and trading systems. Once I knew my system preference, I did mix-and-match of indicators. My Favorite Trading Systems and Favorite Signal chapters have summarized my system findings and closing.

For the first six months, I would recommend a learner to explore different methodologies to establish a basic foundation. We will get to know our preference over time and trials. As an inexperienced Futures learner, please stay with instruments that are not moving very fast. For example, CL (crude oil Futures) is a very advanced instrument. Try it only when we have become more advanced. Always start with simulation.

Let me do a short recap. We all have at least a reason to take a close look on Futures. Regardless of the learning approach or trading strategy we are going to take, please do not trade a live account or risk an investment capital until we have a legitimate profitable performance record on a trading system.

Learn to crawl before we walk. Then learn to run. There are fundamentals such as

How to read a price bar? There are different bar formats. For example, candlesticks, lines and Renko bars. Get to know at least how to read them, including the start and end time of a particular bar. If you are staying with candle sticks, learn how to read bullish/bearish and seller/buyer tails etc.

What are interval settings? Experiment with different interval settings. I tried possibly about 10. For example, minute, range, Renko, volume, regular line and candle sticks.

Beth Fiedler

Learning does not stay with a label name. When I decided to stay with a range chart, I knew exactly why. If we are going to use multiple charts, what is the ideal combo? For my research, I learned that 1:1.5 is appropriate. Say lower time frame chart is 5-Range, then its corresponding higher time frame chart can be 7 to 8-Range.

Another important factor to consider will be the instrument/market. They all have a different personality and volatility level. That's why I have been emphasizing the importance to find a match and spend time to learn different markets' behaviors.

MY SELF-LEARNING JOURNEY

After my eventful live trading week, I reviewed my two trading systems. There was nothing wrong with the entry rules. It was me who triggered the grievances.

I modified my daily game plan with the following strategy and added a list of To-do items.

Want Only What the Market Wants
Trade with the TREND
Only Trade High Probability Trades
Sit On Hands and Wait Patiently For a Signal
Preserve Precious Capital

To-Do Items

- Always check the daily news announcement
- Do not trade when there is important news
- Identify the trend (for example, Up, Down, Choppy, Mixed and Sideway)

Beth Fiedler

Daily Game Plan

No of Trading Systems: 2

- Scalping (Primary system for quick trades)
- Trending (Secondary system to help me to stay with the main trend)

No of Charts: 4
Trading Time: 9:30-11:30 am Eastern Standard Time
Trade Size: 2- to 3-contract trades
Profit Target: 5-6 ticks for the first contract
Second/Last Profit Target: Not defined and let the trade run
Stop Loss: Within 15 ticks from entry

Exit Plan: Exit when there is a warning from one or more of the indicators / Cautious when the price gets close to a major Support/Resistance level

Note: Would not let a winner become a loser.

As an inexperienced trader and a new Futures learner, I continued trading two systems and four charts. I did multiple-contract trades and tried to have a runner. A typical morning I traded over 10 contracts and made over 60 ticks or lost 100 ticks. It was great, right?

Wrong!! Too aggressive for a newbie and my behavior was far from ideal! It was an afterthought and I did not see my aggressiveness until months later.

I created vision cards for my game plan and exit strategy. I had my plan and rules all mapped out and they were posted at my trade station.

There were days when the market was extremely slow and choppy. At the beginning, I often forced a trade hoping to get a few ticks here and there. Losing a few ticks did not scare me. I was on simulation and did not feel the heat or pain when I had a few losing trades or a losing day or even a losing week.

I was not trading sim as if I would be trading live. There were times I placed a 50- or 100-contract trade just for fun and excitement to see my account grew in hundreds of dollars within minutes.

I tested out different indicators every day. Not only was I on a mission to locate a profitable trading system, I was also searching for an indicator or indicators to alert me of choppiness so that I could stay out of the market. I was looking for indicators to provide me with 100% protection. I would never have a losing trade and not even a losing tick.

I worried about being chopped. I tried uncountable indicators that would give me warnings. They saved me entering into some losing trades yet they also stopped me from entering into some winning ones. I have not performed an in-depth analysis. However, my guess is these warning indicators likely end up balancing out most of the time.

When I over-emphasized choppiness and worried too much, I became reluctant to place a trade when all my entry rules aligned. When that particular signal worked out and was a big winner, I beat myself up for not taking it. I could never win!

What is the most effective way to avoid being chopped? If we do not feel comfortable to take a signal for whatever reasons or just one reason (sometimes could be a gut feeling), leave the trade station for a short break. Come back and wait for another signal.

Bear in mind that there will always be high probability setups waiting! The market will always be there!

Scalping

Some trading friends often tease me "I am a quick scalper" – a trader who prefers to be in and out of a trade within minutes. My shortest trade was less than 8 seconds (applicable to both winning and losing trades).

Scalping is a personal preference that better matches my personality. I became very uneasy when a trade lasted for over 15 minutes. I have friends who prefer holding on to a trade for hours or days/weeks.

For example, a few trading friends have a daily game plan to place one trade per day if a signal gets triggered before 12:00 noon. Upon entry, the trade has a predetermined exit time of 5 minutes before the market closes. Some of them do not have a pair of predetermined profit target and stop loss orders. A few have a predetermined stop loss order says US$500 and do not have a predetermined profit target order.

If no trade gets triggered before 12:00 noon, they close down their trade station for the day. If there is a trade going on before 12:00 noon, very often they will leave their trade station and let the trade run its course. They do not monitor their trade like a hawk. It took me months before I could step away from my trade station, especially when I had a trade on.

We will all get to know our trading preferences after experimenting with different trading systems and instruments. Very important to remember: the trader is the one trading the system. Tailor-make it to meet the trader's every need. For example, feel free to adjust the chart's layout and indicators' parameters. I love to have thicker lines for moving averages. Some friends prefer dotted lines. My charts always have a momentum/volatility indicator on a separate panel while some friends cannot part with a volume indicator.

Once I started my learning, it had become a 24/7 job. There were thousands and one thing I need to explore. When I was with two mentors in the option spreads trading room, we were using some minute charts, namely 1-, 15-, 30- and 60-minute ones. When I was in another trading room that traded pullback and breakout signals, we were using volume charts. I will cover my trading room experience in a separate chapter.

Back to the two trading systems I used in early 2010. They were MedianRenko charts. To me, MedianRenko is a tick or range chart.

Those interested in getting a more sophisticated definition please feel free to do a search.

I stayed with the creator's indicators and entry rules as I was too inexperienced and new to make any changes. However, when I found the price movement too fast for me, I adjusted the interval settings.

I first used a 4-tick chart for the scalping system. I changed it to a 6-tick chart to slow down the price action. When I found a 6-tick chart too slow for me, I switched it back to a 4-tick chart. I would recommend at least two weeks before making one to maximum two changes in a trading system.

Some may think they are capable of managing multiple trading systems at the same time. For most it is not advisable. For me, I started with multiple systems, multiple instruments and multiple-contract trades. It took me months to realize my stupidity. I am glad to share my mistakes so that the readers will save both time and resources.

TRADING ROOM EXPERIENCE

When I subscribed to an online option spreads program, it came with a lifetime membership and access to a trading room. It was my first trading room experience. We love freebies and so am I (as always).

As an inexperienced trader, be sure to ask questions. That was how I got connected with a few trading friends who were very generous in sharing their experience with me.

At the beginning, we had two coaches who took turns to run the trading room. Then one left and started his own trading business. I was with the second coach for about three months. He was not willing to share his trading system with us. Simply called out a trade signal and it was up to us to follow or not. I did my first Futures trade and it was a quick winner of four ticks (US$50 before commission).

Most of us also followed his suggestion on directional options, option spreads and Futures. We were supposed to have stop orders for our trades. Unfortunately, we chose to follow his hold suggestion on some losing trades and did not follow an exit plan. I did not recall any trades that we were able to regain any losing ground and instead I lost over 50% of the original investment.

My Roller Coaster Ride

As we did not know what trading system he was using, we all relied on his judgement and followed blindly. I knew it was not sensible. Sometimes we could not think straight, especially when our trades were not working. We followed a supposedly guru, hoping that we would win at the end. When a loss got out of control, we only had ourselves to blame and not the coach.

If the readers wonder why, it was because we were all managing our own trading account. We decided to enter a trade and were also responsible for the exit. It could be difficult to swallow. After losing thousands with that coach, the most important lesson I learned was to have an exit plan for every investment.

I got a recommendation to try a second trading room. This time I was with two trading friends. We did our homework and first started with a one-week trial at a nominal rate. A week was not long enough to tell if a trading room and the moderator were a match for us. Having friends soothed the uncertainty. We decided to go with a quarterly subscription because we got a 25% discount.

We were trading YM (Dow Jones Futures) and the suggested profit target and stop loss were 6 and 20 ticks respectively. Their historical performance record was about 70% profitable. As an inexperienced trader who was desperate to make a part-time income, I counted on more peers' recommendation than exercising my own assessment. I was more like a follower.

Three of us all lost money with this vendor. That was what happened. When a trade was not working, the moderator often added one or more contracts to get a better average price. I seldom added and whenever I did, it was a double-losing trade. My trading friends also suspected that the moderator entered into a trade before calling out a trade. After a few losing weeks, we left the room and started our own.

Warning: It was not a good deal because we ended up leaving within weeks and could not get a refund back on the remaining subscription months.

A trading friend took a lead and ran a room for four of us. We all had a different trading system. I was juggling with two systems, namely a fractal breakout system and one based on my friends' sharing. I was pretty new to Futures trading and did not have the confidence or competence to trade on my own.

The room stayed open almost the whole day. It was like a Monday to Friday job for us. I was not the one pointing out the trend and possible trade signals. I was more waiting for a suggestion and decided if I was going to take a trade or not. There were occasional losers and winners on an inconsistent basis. I started writing daily recaps on trades that I took both on simulation and live. The focus was on how to improve my mental state and performance. Review and reflection were very useful to develop a consistent trading discipline.

To stay in a protective environment, unfortunately, has become an obstacle to my independence. I relied excessively on my peers' suggestion and was not close to becoming a trader on my own. I estimate that those who choose to be in a trading room can be categorized as follows:

Interactive Environment

Some traders have a need to be accompanied and prefer to be in a group. Most rooms allow the users to chat via text which will fulfill their interaction need. I did come across very seasoned traders in paid trading rooms. These experienced traders told me they preferred an interactive trading environment, even they are very competent in trading their system.

Learning Need

Some traders (like me when I was very inexperienced) have a need to count on someone for direction and/or guidance before they develop enough confidence in a system plus more confidence for themselves. In some circumstances, they have the luxury to blame the moderator for a losing trade since the moderator calls out that signal. It represents a potential risk to develop a parasite habit and the traders will not learn to take full responsibility for their trade performance.

There are pros and cons and really depend on the trader's personality and more the reason behind joining a trading room. For guidance and support as a start is reasonable. Yet they must be cautious in developing a parasite habit and start shifting their responsibility.

Luckily, I seldom blame anyone except myself. I am the one solely responsible for my account performance. I am the one who presses a button to enter and exit a trade.

The main drawback to my friends' trading room was I became a burden to my trading friends. They worried about my losing money when the signals they called out were losers. When I relied heavily on my friends, I was not learning to trade on my own.

I was in several other trading rooms. Not for long. Some lasted for a few days and some lasted for a few weeks. After trying two paid vendors and both were unsuccessful, I lost confidence in trying more until I got tempted again by a trading friend's recommendation.

The trading system was based on price action. The vendor was hosting a short briefing session during lunch break every trading day. Free access to their trading room with live charts on.

I studied their trading system for some weeks and got a complimentary old version from a trading forum. When I started my Futures learning, I was lucky and came across many resources that offered complimentary products and services. Most have become obsolete or require subscription when I visited their websites this year.

Back to that particular trading system and free trading room. I was almost getting to trade the system live. The only drawback I experienced was false breakouts and low reward/risk ratio (less than 1:1). The market movement was very narrow. The suggested profit target and stop loss did not meet my expectation.

In summer 2010, I was trading crude oil Futures for about two months. Need to warn the readers that crude oil Futures is a very fast market and more suitable for experienced traders. The first month I familiarized myself with a trading system and the crude oil Futures market. The system is still the simplest method that I have tried so far. I automated the entry rules so that when the market conditions were in place, my trading strategy would plot a pair of potential trades on the chart. I also created an automated trading strategy with a pair of predetermined profit target and stop loss orders. I could activate my strategy and run it in simulation or live account.

I traded the system manually on my live account for a month. I was in a trading room with some friends who were trading the same system. It was more for rapport and it did help developing my confidence.

It was a profitable experience because the profitability of the system was over 80% based on its historical performance. Why I stopped after a month of live trading? The suggested stop loss was huge and the reward/risk ratio was 1:3, ie profit target of eight ticks and stop loss of 24 ticks or higher. One big loser at the end of the month wiped out two-third of the accumulated profit.

There was no way to safeguard losing trades. We all know that. If we try to justify and/or give reasons for not taking a signal, very often it would turn out to be a winner. Then we felt bad missing a winner. However, when we decided to take a signal and it turned out to be a big loser, we were not getting anywhere. Since I was not mentally prepared to accept occasional big losers, the only alternative was to find another trading system.

In Fall 2010, I tried another trading room. See, I did try close to 10. What attracted me to this trading room was its trading system. It was very simple compared to the ones I created myself for the same time span.

My trading system consisted of two charts (lower and higher time frames) and had almost 10 indicators on each. That trading system consisted of one chart and only had two moving averages and a momentum indicator on it. Its entry rules were based on the price movement and were very easy to follow.

That system was an eye-opening experience for me. I could never imagine one could trade their real money with such a simple system. Of course, I have trading friends who do not use any indicators and place trades based on price movement only. Some of us teased them trading "naked". I watched a few videos and it was more on how confident the traders are at interpreting the price movement. Like many other trading systems, they branch out and you can easily find different methodologies on trading "naked".

I started trading that system on my live account and simulation. The good news was I did not lose much. The bad news was I was still under the illusion that I could safeguard losing trades and became unnecessarily choosy. I also started to learn Fibonacci levels as the moderator shared his knowledge on the critical Fibonacci levels and how they aligned with the signals.

I had a tendency to complicate things and I did again. I spent hours in research and watched hours of videos on Fibonacci. My head was so stuffed that I was lost as to what do next. Luckily I paused and came to an agreement with myself that I only needed to understand the basics. Then I had an internal dialogue with myself as to why and what triggered this goose-hunt again?

It was a simple answer. I was not confident and felt incompetent to trade. What can I do to fill this gap? I started writing down the entry rules of my favorite setups. Very specific I must add and I picked a financial instrument that I was committed to trade on simulation.

I logged on my trading platform and created a chart with four months historical data. Tabulated all the signals (over 120) matching my entry rules on a spreadsheet. The next step was to validate the system's performance and expectancy with details such as

- Probability of Win
- Probability of Loss
- Winning Trades Produced
- Losing Trades Produced
- Average Winning Trade
- Average Losing Trade
- Net Profit

The overall expectancy would enhance our understanding of the system's performance in different aspects. In most circumstances, the above breakdown would identify areas the traders could work on to bring up the performance level. For example, an earlier exit (to save a few ticks) may lower the average losing trade. I cover how to validate a system's performance and tabulate expectancy on two different chapters.

I started sim-trading a system with a plan to complete 50 trades within weeks. It took me more time, even I was on the simulator. Ego and pride were the reasons why I was reluctant in taking signals that matched my entry rules.

Upon completion of my 50-trade assignment, I got sidetracked and joined some trading friends' chat room. It was challenging to resist their offer when they told me they had a profitable and simple trading system.

I had some crazy weeks. I acted as if I was a super-machine that could function 24/7. A normal day was getting up around 2:00 am in the morning as London session starts at 2:30-3:00 am. Paused around 5:30 am when it was close to their lunch break. Then resumed around 7:00 am when we might have some pre-US market movement. I did not want to miss anything. Then a lunch break between 12:00 noon and 1:00 pm. I was watching the market like a hawk up to 4:00 pm. Back to an evening market around 7:00 pm when some Asian markets got active up to 10:00 pm.

To do a simple math, I had less than 10 inactive market hours and very often I would be testing out indicators, creating strategies or going through the price movement and figured out why I had missed some great setups. All winning signals that I failed to take were good signals.

These were the craziest weeks of my trading life. I had four monitors filled with over 10 financial instruments and over 20 charts. I was monitoring these markets concurrently. Some charts might be minimized when I tried to focus on 3-5 instruments, but I could not resist maximizing them when my trading friends told us they just did this and that. I was also using almost five if not more trading systems at the same time. It was again a bad habit trying to have a holy grail with a 100% win guarantee.

When I was using multiple systems to validate a signal, I missed good trade signals most of the time. I did not know why I got myself into an illusion that I could make it work.

I came out of this dilemma with relief and realization that simplicity would always be the most critical success factor in my trading. At the end whether we decide to stay or leave trading, we must get certain things straight and I had them spelled out in this book.

It is my every intention to share my experience with a goal to make the readers' life easier and pain-free. I will follow what I preached here should I have to start all over again. It will no longer be an 8-year working assignment and they will get a breakthrough within a year or two. They will be in a good position to decide if trading is for them.

More importantly, before starting a trading venture, they will perform ongoing review and reflection to assess their progress and decide whether they want to continue.

When I was with this group of trading friends, I got to know about another trading room. They were all impressed by the moderator who could specify exactly where to enter and quite often won. It was a system with an 80% winning rate. Profit target and stop loss were 4 to 3-4 ticks respectively. Considering a small stop loss which was affordable, I gave it a try.

I subscribed to three months again because it was cheaper than the monthly term. You will know soon if I made a good choice.

Room subscription did not include the system. It was quite sophisticated with at least 10 indicators on and we were looking at multiple charts and two financial instruments. The systems and indicators were available for purchase. For me, they were quite expensive and I stayed with my own.

For the first week, I had to familiarize myself with the moderator's speaking style and vocabularies. I sim-traded his signals when I could interpret his instructions correctly. When I got to the third week, I started trading his signals live.

Temptation won and I did not observe a disciplined trader's code of conduct. I made the following mistakes:

- I did not have the patience to sim-trade at least 50 signals (ideally 100 signals)
- I did not prepare a performance record of the sim-traded signals to validate my own performance and the system performance

- I did not have the system to tabulate its expectancy and profitability before my sim- and live-trading (win 80% were hearsay)
- I did not have a checklist for my favorite setup (I had to confess that I was not even using the system and how could I accomplish this requirement?)

What was the worst mistake I made when I was with this vendor? I was not even using his system! I was constantly in mental clashes, especially when my own system conflicted with his. For example, he alerted us that he was looking for a buy opportunity at a particular price level. My system indicated selling only.

I was unable to trade his signals profitably because I was doing only one-contract trades and maximum two trades a day. Even his stop loss was only 3-4 ticks, after one or two losing trades, I was out because I reached my daily stop loss. If we had a winner, I would only be making four ticks. At the end of the first two weeks, my weekly performance was 6-10 ticks in red. Unless and until I was willing to do multiple-contract trades which I was not prepared to, this 80% profitable system would not work for me.

I left the room after a month. I did not try to get a refund for the last two months. Nothing wrong with his system and it was a mismatch. Having said that, I did learn some valuable lessons from the moderator. For example,

I must know what I am doing. Using the same trading system in a trading room should be a must because different systems behave differently at different timelines. Multiple systems would definitely trigger unnecessary conflicts and stress not to mention confusion. The moderator demonstrated ease and calm in managing his trades. He had a trading plan for all trades inclusive of different exit points for his multiple-contract trades. I admired his discipline and do not regret subscribing to his room.

Do I have more trading room experience? I did. I visited at least three more trading rooms. Not shopping for a trading system and more about how traders managed their trade.

Beth Fiedler

After trying hundreds of indicators and systems, I realize it is not about the trading system we use to trade, it is definitely more of the traders and their trade management skills!

EXPECTATION VERSUS REALITY

WHAT TO EXPECT?

Learn how to trade is demanding and the readers can tell from the book. For those who follow the suggestion on the book, they stand a better chance to remain healthy both physically and mentally. Be careful that there will always be a little voice to tell us to do more. Mine was very loud and it encouraged me to keep searching and trying.

I took my Futures learning very seriously and turned it into 24/7. Under-capitalized status had added more stress and anxiety as well. I appreciated the tips from more experienced traders who reminded me to lead a healthy lifestyle. I did try and not very successful in the first two years. Until I got settled with a simple system, my life finally got back to more normal.

Whether trading is going to be a part- or full-time job or business, let's get the readers prepared for a fun and educational journey. There are always things we can do. Keep a good journal and be sure to throw in a review and reflection column.

When I went through my journals and notebooks (I had about six thick ones with my scribbles), I could giggle at things and thoughts that I wrote. They were treasures and great life experience that helped my growth and molded who I have become.

We all have different agenda items. Once we have guidance on where to start, an uncertain venture does not look dim or scary anymore. For those who have some rough ideas on what to expect and stay with a trading plan with commitment, they will be way ahead thousands.

Our biggest enemy will always be ourselves. Our pride and ego will take us to detour to fulfil our hope for a successful fast track. We are only humans and especially when we feel not getting anywhere. No worries as long as we can afford the time and resources. We will learn something from these mishaps.

Once we are back on track, stay focused and continue our learning. It does not hurt trying as long as they are affordable and will not trigger any serious mental and financial damages to us and/or those around us.

I strongly oppose to borrow funds in order to learn how to trade or do real trades. This warning applies even we thought we had a profitable trading system that passes the assessment process with flying colors.

First, we will be trading with scary money, not an investment capital that we can afford to lose. Second, trading live is completely different from trading on a simulator or market replay or plot through historical charts. We must take time and adjustment to switch over to live trading.

Most of us tie our trading performance with our personal performance. Trading is not about losing face and brag about how profitable we are. We must have a proper attitude to understand why we want to trade. Find a way to detach our personal performance and emotion with trading.

For me, becoming mechanical serves me well. I no longer feel lost after a losing trade, a losing day or even a losing week. As long as I follow my plan and checklist to identify my favorite signals, I am content with the trade result.

Will most get bored with a routine that supposedly to last forever? Some will and cannot resist checking out new indicators and systems. I am no different. When I come across a new indicator and system these days, I will still put it on for a day or two. Most systems point out the same trade and a signal at the same time or with a slight variation and time lapse. Until we are willing to go through the whole validation process again, we may as well save some time and continue with the existing system.

When there are changes on the market, culture, trend and financial instrument, it will be the right time to do a more serious system revamp. Until then, I am content with a system that has passed the validation process and I feel comfortable to trade it live.

BLACK HOLE

When I was working diligently on my Futures venture, very often I felt like I was in a black hole. It was a figurative place of emptiness and loneliness. I was trapped in a region of space with an intense gravitational field and there was no escape route.

Of course if I chose to quit, it was an escape route for me. Like I mentioned before, quitting is not an option unless I am running out of resources and strength to continue. Having said that, I do not encourage fruitless attempts to stay on a mission that is not compatible with one's lifestyle. I must confess that if I did not have a breakthrough in early 2011, quitting could be an option for me.

To be in a black hole sounds scary! Why most choose to stay for years (not months in most cases)? Based on my experience, hope and pride are often the reasons to keep us there.

There are hundreds or even thousands of new systems and indicators entering into the market on a regular basis. For those (like me) on dozens of distribution lists, they will be receiving "hopeful" emails every day with eye-catching headlines.

I have not subscribed to their paid services. Yet most of these vendors offer complimentary introduction sessions which continue keeping the subscribers hopeful that they would design and/or find a profitable trading system soon.

For me, there were uncountable moments that I thought I was very close to trade a profitable system. Then a blow! It was a recurring cyclone for me. I was surprised that my petite heart was strong enough to overcome the unexpected blows one after another. I am lucky to be a positive person who can always find a way to comfort my defeated morale.

I shared my 6Ws very often in this book and they are not trading-specific. I truly believe to succeed in anything and everything, having the wisdom to specify 6Ws helps. Last but not least, we need the encourage to admit and accept what is the best for us both physically, mentally and financially.

That's what this book is about. To enlighten those who may consider day trading Futures. To invest a few months or up to a year to accomplish the basics as outlined in the book. Those who take time and make a commitment to do that; they will be in a better position to make a sensible decision on the next move. I am confident that this book will save the readers hundreds of hours and thousands of dollars.

My recommendation is to enjoy the learning process. It is going to be an eye-opening and inspiring life experience. Futures trading could be an uncertain item in their mind for years. Considering the risks it poses, most have been reluctant to pursue it. Now that with some guidance provided in this book, it is time to make a move. I went through the cost of learning procrastination in the Call For Action chapter.

No need to worry too much about the financial outcome because the readers will become more informed about the cost. Those who decide to start the learning process, I am confident that they will get to know themselves better. For me, my Futures learning was a life-changing event.

I have become a better person in many ways. For example,

- I have become more patient with others
- I have become more considerate of others' needs
- I learn to give myself more time to think and re-position
- I learn to be more flexible and become more apt to change
- I have become a more sensitive person to acknowledge my personal needs

I said quitting has never been an option in my life. Having experienced what I experienced in trading, I believe I have the ability to execute a quitting decision when it is a right thing to do.

It is always a challenge for our head, mind and heart to align. Trading has definitely turned me into a more sensitive person with a bigger heart and more persistence. I considered myself an organized person. Yet trading has turned me into a more visionary person with better discipline and courage to admit failure and deficiency. I used to have a big ego. No more after years of Futures learning and trading. I still have an ego, but more bendable and flexible with a limit.

I sincerely hope that most do not need to spend years of time and resources (which I did) on their Futures learning. If they choose to, after going through a fast track that I proposed, it is a more informed decision.

Trading is always a serious business and we badly wanted it to work for us. Yet most of us started trading without getting ourselves prepared physically, mentally and financially on how demanding trading could be!

TIME WARP

When I said I was in a time warp, I meant I was living in an illusion in which time appeared to stand still. I thought I was in good progress. Very often excitement and success were short-lived. I was back to where I was and sometimes could be worse in a way that I felt I had to start everything all over again.

For me, started all over was not an issue. The challenge was the start-over was recurring once every few weeks. I was in a constant struggle as to what to use for my trading system or what trading system should I use to trade my live account.

I tried hundreds of indicators and created over a hundred of automated trading strategies. Was it possible to incorporate all or most of them into one trading system? I never thought of doing that. However, I did strive to have as many indicators as I could possibly have on my system. "More" to me meant more protection and could save me from losing money.

Until I accepted losing trades in my trading life, I was in a time warp where I continuously revamped and made changes to my systems. Of course I was testing different indicators and systems all the time.

Beth Fiedler

How did I break the time warp spell? Instead of reviewing and revamping my trading system, I had more review and reflection on myself.

Trading is more about the trader! Until a trader realizes that and starts looking within, everything stands still and time warp persists!

JUSTIFY EVERY MOVE?

Do we need a reason or reasons to justify every move? We all want to win and make money. Whether we are on simulation or trading live, most of us have a tendency to justify every trade decision. This applies to a losing trade and surprisingly a winning trade that does not align with the trading rules as well.

It was very tiring for me! A winning trade that did not align with the trading rules and yet was a winner. It was detrimental to my development and that was exactly what happened!

First, I started having doubts about my trading system. Second, it encouraged me to disobey the entry rules I created. Third, I became more disoriented and wanted to be on free fly again.

When I spent more time in justifying every trade decision I made, I was building more obstacles for my discipline development. When I wanted to be right for every trade, I still had a personal attachment to them. I took it personally and a trade result reflected my success and failure. It became a big ego issue for me.

I wanted to be right all the time. Yet trading is a different game. It is definitely not about right or wrong. Not the trader anyway. To develop and pursue a successful trading career, it is more on creating a solid foundation of a disciplined trader. Discipline means following rules. It is very important to get the sequence and priority right.

Beth Fiedler

As long as I follow the predetermined entry rules which I created, there is no need to justify every move. When I stopped arguing on every trade decision, I became more comfortable in trading my system.

SYSTEM (SOUL) SEARCH

We all have a tendency to hope for better or the best. Hope will convince us to continue our system search and/or modify our trading system on an ongoing basis.

It is extremely dangerous if we unknowingly stay in a search and forget about time. I was in that trap for months. Never-ending trials on different systems and indicators. My behavior was very addictive and I was out-of-control. I got lucky that I paused and eventually stopped my search. It took an extra amount of efforts and reminders.

What will be the consequences if we cannot stop? We will spend years in research and non-stop system enhancement. We will stay satisfied with a system for a short period of time (usually less than a month) before casting doubts on our favorite signals. Then we started making changes to our system hoping to improve its performance. It is going to be a continuous loop. Very often there is no end to it. I was in a forever system search spell and it was heartbroken not to mention the time I spent.

I have friends who have spent years on their system search and are still in their development stage. They have been telling me that they are very close to complete designing their perfect system. They will recover their former losses and their so-called perfect system is their ticket to financial freedom.

Beth Fiedler

I also have friends who continue adding more rules and sophisticated features to their system. They knew there is no holy grail yet they cannot stop trying to create one that is close to be a holy grail.

I feel sad because they would get nowhere except spending more time and resources on a fruitless goose hunt. I do not have the heart to tell them to stop and instead focus on a system that they can trade on a consistently profitable basis.

Trading success is not about trading a perfect system (which does not exist anyway). Trading success is about building consistency and confidence over time. Trading success is more about money and trade management. It took me a long time to realize this!

WHAT DID I WANT?

I was totally attracted by these popular pitches when I first started my Futures trading:

Secret to never losing a trade
Post-learning Comments: Traders need to accept losing. Or else forget about trading!

Automatically find you guaranteed profit opportunities
Post-learning Comments: There is no guarantee. Trading is not for those who are looking for guaranteed profit opportunities!

Low risk and without any hassle
Post-learning Comments: Trading is about high risk with uncertainties. Those who cannot accept this hard reality please do not trade!

Once I started placing live Futures trades, I came to a dawning realization that losing is and will always be inevitable in trading! Different investment options come with different risk levels. For example, conservative traders may choose to invest in a financial instrument that comes with a guaranteed return on investment. I did that before. It was quite disappointing when the accumulated multiple-year guaranteed return was not sufficient to cover the incurred inflation. Having said that, those conservative investment options did protect my investment principal 100%.

As we get closer to our retirement, some of us cannot resist an urge to investigate other options. Time is the currency for the 21st century. Time is also an intangible asset with opportunity costs as well. I agree that a head start with investing is advisable. When we have more years before retirement, we "may" be in a better position to recover from a cyclical downturn of the financial markets. Pay attention please to "may"!

We can all go through decades of historical performance on most financial markets and instruments. Some of us will see a pattern, but there is no guarantee of a smooth profit curve. Can we tell when to enter and exit based on historical performance or a particular market's behavior? Unfortunately, not for most of us.

When I had a time factor of 20-40 years before retirement, I used to think that my investment would and could recover over time. Having experienced three market clashes within a 20-year timeline, I am now with a camp that does not recommend long-term holding especially after a big crash.

As I mentioned in the FINANCIAL PLANNING section, all investments (regardless of the instrument and market in question) must always have a predetermined exit plan before placing a trade. Once an investment is on, the trader must follow an exit plan either to cash in some profits or cut loss. Should I have such an exit plan in place years ago, I could have saved close to US$100,000. Since I was stupid enough not to exit from most of my investments and held on to a belief that my investments would gradually regain their lost ground, I had no one to blame except myself. I was buying mostly blue chips with every intention to hold them for decades. I have held them forever, ie until most of them were 100% write-off or for a few instances I exited with 5-10% principal back to my trading account.

There were bounce-back investments (not the ones I held) giving them some years. Will a "Forever Hold" strategy work if one has both time and resources? I do not know and possibly no one knows. It is a guessing game.

Having lost a small fortune in different financial markets over the years, it has always been "hope" that brought me back to the market and invested again on different instruments every time. Could be just me out-of-luck. Nevertheless, I have become a more informed and sensible investor. I know how to protect my capital and have a better understanding of my risk and what to expect. However, I no longer believe in a "Forever Hold" strategy.

The market structure has changed over time. For those who have an extended timeline plus an investment is a very strong one, I will still recommend an exit plan for better protection. Sensible investors are better off with an exit plan.

Yes, I am a strong believer in having a predetermined profit target and stop loss orders for all investments. I have covered my recommendation on the ACTION PLAN and FINANCIAL PLANNING sections.

The suggested investment portfolio is adaptable and depends on the investor's trading style and risk level. The listed categories are for illustration purposes only. Some may opt-in and some will opt-out. Some may not end up with multiple instruments on their trading plan. It does not matter. The time you spend on creating your trading plan and daily game plan will be beneficial for educational purposes. It will give you an opportunity to familiarize yourself with some options out there (not an entire list). You may not consider investing in them today. You can always re-visit some of them at a later date. It is inevitable that we will change over time and look at the same investment options differently at a different timeline.

I know some have been adopting an "Invest and Forget" strategy on a small portion of their investment portfolio. For me, I feel comfortable to allocate up to 20% of my available investment funds to long-term variable or fixed term securities (up to 10 years). It has been giving me a comfortable feeling that at least my investment portfolio is partially protected. I imagine not all traders need that.

SAME TRADING SYSTEM GENERATES DIFFERENT TRADING RESULTS?

When I was in a profitable trading room, I thought I would always be profitable. The readers can tell from the Trading Room Experience chapter that it was not true. When I was using a trading system that was profitable for my trading friends, I thought I would be profitable as long as I followed the entry rules diligently. Wrong again.

We could be using the same trading system. We could be using the same system to trade the same financial instrument. We could be using the same system to trade the same financial instrument at the same time. We could even be in the same trade at the same time. Yet our trades would and could generate different trading results. Why?

First, our trading plans differ!
Second, our trading management skills differ!
Third, our trading preferences differ!
Fourth, traders are different!

Let me elaborate with the following real trade experience:

Beth
Profit Target 6 / Stop Loss 6

Trading Friend #1
Profit Target 80 / Stop Loss 30 (Adjust Stop Loss to break even after reaching 40 ticks of profit)

Trading Friend #2
Profit Target and Stop Loss Nil (Exit 5 minutes before the market closes)

We entered into a trade based on the same trading system. Yet we had been generating trading results every time. There are no rights and wrongs here. When both trading friends #1 and #2 made more ticks, I admired their courage and strength to stay in a trade longer than me plus having the ability to resist cashing in a profitable trade before hitting their exit condition. I am always a scalper and my trade often ends within minutes. The shortest trade completed within 8 seconds! The most important lesson for me was I developed my own trading plan and I am responsible for every trading decision.

Another point worth noting is how we manage a trade. For those who do not have enough confidence in a trading system or themselves or lack of real-time trade management experience, very often they opt out for an early exit, especially when a trade was against them at the very beginning. After an early exit, that trade reversed and ended up a winner reaching their profit target. They often beat themselves up for not staying in that trade. This happened to me many times until I became more disciplined and stayed with my daily game rules.

It is easier said than done. It will definitely take time to develop some disciplined trader's traits. I strongly urge the readers to take note that a trader's behavior overrides the importance of a trading system. We all think, react and process the same information differently. How could we expect the same result from two different traders!

Additional comments on hardware and physical environment differences:

- Physical location (check your computer's ping rate – traders who are closer to the Exchange getting their orders filled first)
- Computer's processing speed
- Internet connection strength
- Broker's trading platform
- Trade entry time (seconds or even milliseconds make a difference)
- What applications are running on the computer

BREAKTHROUGH

TRADING IS A BUSINESS

Most will think twice before starting a new business. Anyone who intends to trade is highly recommended to consider trading as a business plus more. Running a successful business requires dedication, time and resources. Having a correct frame of mind will give the readers a great head-start on trading!

Not only do we need to cushion operating expenses inclusive of a back-up plan which I cover in the On Your Mark, Get Set, BEFORE Go chapter, we must also be prepared to run a trading business with specific operation hours and resources.

Start and run a business will incur an operation cost though some business owners do not cushion any basic compensation for their time and services for the first few years. Trading is a business, whether the traders are going to operate on a part- or full-time basis. I categorized the must-have skill sets to start a trading business as follows:

Language Skill

The traders must be proficient to understand the markets, financial instruments, trading systems, indicators and trading platforms that they are going to trade. Having an ambiguous language barrier will add more stress, anxiety and uncertainty to their trading lives.

Computer Skill

The traders must feel confident and competent to operate and manage their trading platform, trading system and trades. They must be self-sufficient in setting up their system on a trading platform of their choice. They must be extremely efficient in completing a trade from entry to exit.

Learning Skill

The traders must have a humble and open learning attitude. If they think they knew everything and are always quick at learning anything, be prepared for many "nice" surprises.

Listening Skill

Please put your ears and eyes on duty. I came across many learners who were reluctant and resistant to read and listen. For example, most showed up at an education session without setting up their audio/video facilities when the setup instructions were included in the registration email.

Note: It was a 20-second setup process. If there was a prep exercise involved, over 50% did not complete it before attendance. In most circumstances, they had hundreds and one reasons for not doing this and that. If you do not have the time, the most sensible decision will be to put it aside. There is no point of starting when your heart is only half in it.

Crisis Management Skill

Trading is a very demanding activity, especially on a psychological aspect. Explore ways to enhance our mental skills so that we will always maintain a peaceful state of mind. This is useful for leading a harmonious lifestyle as well.

Reading Skill

Love to read will certainly bring more joy to the learning process.

Trading is not for those who do not have time or a strong commitment to make things happen. Hundreds approached me for advice and most never took action on educating themselves on trading. Some continued adding more sophisticated indicators to their trading systems. I remembered seeing some charts with overwhelming indicators on them. They were so complicated that I believe only a few can understand them after investing months to digest the information. I committed the same crime before and it was really scary when we indulged ourselves in such a web-like mess.

Some did not realize without a dispensable investment capital, they would not be fit for trading of any kind. We had subscribers who urged for special discounts as they cannot afford a monthly subscription of US$100. We had subscribers who requested an installment plan for a quarterly subscription of US$240. We had subscribers who were on social welfare programs and wanted to trade their daily meal funds. Some subscribers would be mentally and financially stressed if they had a losing trade of US$50.

Believe me! They are definitely not ideal candidates for trading. They can use their free time to learn. There are free indicators and trading systems out there. Until they can save an investment capital that they can lose without losing sleep, live trading should not be part of their life.

For those who consider trading as a hobby, my recommendation "Trading is a business" stays true for this group. If they are serious about trading even it is going to be a hobby, they should still consider what I recommended in this book.

IT IS A MIND GAME

I will not recommend to anyone to consider trading as a game. Trading is a serious business, whether it is going to be part-time or full-time. Most of us when we are new to trading, we think it will only be fun making money. No stress or anxiety. If we are serious about trading for a living, we will behave weird even when we are on simulation with sim $ at stake.

I only have a few trading friends who can trade at ease. Some of us (not all I have to warn the readers) will get to that carefree stage with hard work and a consistent trading discipline.

What lured me into trading was how easy it sounded in order to make money with trading. I signed up for almost all free offers that came my way. I have been receiving 30+ emails daily from different vendors trying to sell me their products and services. When I was very inexperienced to trading, especially the first six to twelve months, I was reading pages of reports and sales pitches to gain more knowledge on different financial markets every day.

Quite often I opted to trade some cheap stocks and options based on their recommendation. Almost all were losers and most were 100% write-offs as well. Considering myself an intelligent person, why I continued making non-sensible investment choices? Greed and ignorance plus I was desperate to make some money.

I just got married and relocated to a small city that offered no job opportunities. I had some savings and thought I could generate a part-time income while figuring out what to do.

I did not realize the importance of having a trading plan and a good understanding of my investment capital. An investment capital is the amount that I could afford to lose without triggering any financial issues. I did not know that until I read a trading book.

For the worst scenario, be prepared to lose 100% of the investment capital. I demonstrated how to tabulate one's investment capital in the FINANCIAL PLANNING section. Before making an investment, we must find out if we do have an investment capital (how much) and are mentally and financially prepared to lose it.

If we do not have an investment capital, stop investing and start saving! If we have an investment capital and are willing to part with it 100%, answer the following question honestly:

Will I lose sleep after a losing trade (regardless of the amount)?

We know ourselves better than anyone. If the answer is Yes, stop investing in anything. If trading will bring along mental stress or anxiety to our life, it is not worth pursuing.

If the readers are willing to give trading a try, make sure they go through the whole book and are committed to follow most of the recommendations. I bet they will do research and start reading blogs and threads as well.

Commitment will be our ally and enemy at the same time. If we find ourselves procrastinating or have a strong urge to trade live, pause and start all over again. Unless we are amongst the minority who can afford to lose a substantial amount of money with no sweat, we do need time and resources to develop a sound and solid trading profile.

It is likely to be a long journey for most, including myself. To look at it positively, we will get to know some nice people, we will fall many times, our ego will be bruised, yet we will become a better person in different aspects. When we look back, there will be regrets and valuable life experience as well. That's how I see it!

As time passed by, trading became a mental game for me. I lived and breathed this sport (yes, I called trading a sport) and trading was a very consuming career too. Less than 10% of the traders are successful. I knew it was going to be challenging. I struggled for months and was not prepared for the mental challenges I was constantly facing.

I often thought I was more than halfway through and can smell and taste success. When it turned out to be a fake hope, I began to beat myself up mentally. It was easy to think in hindsight – all the Why questions I started to ask myself. It was no surprise that I started to get negative. I had an Alert chapter in this book.

Trading and learning how to trade would turn us negative. Once we know the trap is out there, we are better equipped to safeguard it. When I was in this sport for months with very high expectations on myself, it could get ugly both mentally and physically when things started to go sour.

Rock Bottom

I was on this journey alone, even Nelson my husband was there for me. There were times I was very upset with myself and extremely upset with my trading performance. All I wanted to do was to complete my learning, no more system/indicator search, and start trading live!

Nelson has been my biggest supporter and I felt like I had let him down. I had never in my life actually been so depressed, at least not for an extended period of time. When I was in my trading venture, feeling hopeless and disappointed was a norm.

Negativity was never in my life dictionary. When I caught myself with this emotion, I quickly corrected myself and continued my pursuit with a positive thought. Negativity would never do anyone, including myself, any good!

How to be a winner out of this mind game? Patience and perseverance! When it is time to make a sensible decision, make it and move on! Always feel good about where we are (even it may not be where you want to be). Negativity itself is a bad thing, but sometimes it can take a "negative" experience to help us realize some important things. As long as we learn from every experience, negative or positive, we will continue to become a better person and get closer to our goal.

DO WE HAVE A MATCH?

I repeatedly mentioned the importance of a match between a trader and his/her trading plan. When assessing a trading plan, every attempt will be made to detect any incongruence and mismatches. For example,

Trading Time: 6:00-8:00 am Eastern Standard Time

We all know the above two-hour time span seldom gives us enough volatility. We need volatility to trade! First, it is lunch break of the London market. Second, important news often comes out around 8:00-8:30 am. We are supposed to sit on hands at least 15 minutes before and after an important news. A quick tabulation of the suggested trading time span does not leave the traders too much quality trading time.

There are certain hours when the market is extremely slow and low volume (says lunch break). If our trading time falls into an inactive zone, we could easily be tempted to take signals that are not classified as high probability ones. We enter into a trade just because we are running out of time.

Bear in mind that we always trade according to real-time price action and the market condition. If we add an unnecessary time constraint to our trading, we very likely commit over-trading when a signal is not there. Very often we make up stories to justify a trade. It was so true based on my own experience.

I have friends who have a full-time job. They only have an hour or two to trade, either before they leave for work or during their lunch break. Some are on Central Time (an hour behind the Eastern Standard Time). They can trade between 7:00 am and 8:30 am Eastern Standard Time. Unfortunately, this 1.5 hour time slot falls during London market's lunch break and before the US market opens at 9:30 am. As I mentioned earlier, we often have important news and data coming out at 8:00-8:30 am. They do not really have enough quality time to trade when a market offers them both volume and volatility.

What did I suggest to them? After considering their geographical location and time zone, I ended up suggesting them to try out the evening market between 7:00-10:00 pm Eastern Standard Time.

Some modified their daily game rules and started simulation in 1-2 financial instruments that have enough volume and volatility in the evening. My biggest challenge to trade at night has been the market's pace. Evening traders definitely need more patience. Waiting time for a signal to materialize will be longer plus a trade cycle from entry to exit will be extended as well.

I personally have not traded an evening market, though I did spend some months monitoring a few financial instruments that were tradable with enough volatility and volume at night. To complete an evening trade can take an hour or more.

For me, I do not have the patience and nerves to sit and wait for an exit order to get filled. Staying in a trade longer than 15 minutes would trigger substantial amount of stress and anxiety on me. If I am going to trade an evening market, I must train myself to feel comfortable to leave a pair of exit orders (profit target and stop loss) unattended and leave my trade station. Until then, evening trading is not for me.

A few trading friends who reside in the Pacific Time zone (three hours behind the Eastern Standard Time) have been getting up at 5:00 am their time to trade for an hour or two as they prefer trading between 8:00-10:00 am Eastern Standard Time. If they do not need to rush to work after an early morning session, it will be doable as they can go back to sleep after trading.

For those who need to shorten their sleep to 4-5 hours/day in order to trade before going to work, I often recommend them to consider other financial instruments that better match their time zone. My concern is the lack of sleep on a regular basis may have a negative impact on our health. Making an additional trading income (which is an uncertainty I must point out) in exchange of health is not a good deal for me.

In addition to a compatible trading time zone, it is also very important to trade a financial instrument whose tick size matches our preference. The good news is there are many choices to keep us entertained.

For me, I have tried US$5, US$10 and US$12.50 per tick size. I was once tempted to trade a European Futures at EUR12.50 per tick. I could not overcome a psychological barrier that it was 25% more than US$ plus the market was too volatile for my liking.

Some of you may laugh at me. I held on to losing trades for 30 points (=120 ticks) or more. A 25% currency exchange difference should be nothing. Your argument is valid. I made many unforgiving trading mistakes and I am not going to repeat them or commit new ones!

PERFECT MATCH

Start with a list of features and highlight the must-haves and nice-to-haves. Most of us could be lost at the beginning because there are hundreds and thousands of systems and indicators available. We will build up more experience and confidence as time passes by. It does not harm to try as many as we want (subject to a predetermined timeline I must add).

It is inevitable to feel overwhelmed and overloaded for the first few months. We probably have a tendency to go for more and not less. That was exactly what happened to me. The first few systems I tried were multi-chart ones plus having over 10 indicators on each chart. Some vendors did not really provide any guidance on their systems. It was like flying on the go for me.

For example, I was in a trading room and the moderator kept shooting us screenshots when the new subscribers (including myself and two friends) did not have a basic understanding of his system. I have to add that I watched over 50 video clips and still did not get it.

Whether a system is complicated or simple, try to prepare a checklist on how to identify a high probability setup. Without a checklist and instead using a hit-or-miss strategy (including guesses) will not work too well. Trading is always about consistency. Minimize guesswork helps eliminate uncertainty, stress and anxiety. As long as we follow predetermined rules, everything else is not important.

It is very likely that inexperienced learners will start with a long list. Then trim it down to less than ten over time. When we have very precise and clear instructions on how to identify high probability signals, we are getting close to draft an action plan. Once we have a shortlisted trading system, focus on learning and understanding one setup will be the most effective (I often call my favorite Triple-A signals).

For inexperienced traders, most will not have their own indicators and trading systems for the first few months. Trade some readily available systems and experiment with free indicators will be a good start. Expose to different methodologies and experience with different systems until we know our system preference.

Start modifying an existing system to meet our personal preference. We will feel more accomplished and polished after several rounds. Once we have a tradable system (must pass the validation process as outlined in the ACTION PLAN section), we are getting closer and closer to our "soul" mate!

It is fine to add our personal preferences to make a system a better fit for us. There are no rights or wrongs here. We are all unique.

TURNED INTO A MECHANICAL TRADER

I took time to train and turn myself into a mechanical trader. It has been working for me because it eliminates over 90% of the emotional decision making process. The following will come in handy if the readers want to give it a try.

Checklist on My Favorite Signal

I prepared a checklist of the entry rules of my favorite signal. Before placing a trade, I manually checked off each and every entry rule. No exception!

With practice and commitment, it took me less than a week to automate the check-off process in my head. Once it was internalized, I executed the process without any personal interpretation on a signal.

Record of 100 Signals

To increase my confidence in the trading system, I tabulated the most recent 100 signals on the instrument I was going to trade. I went through some historical charts and recorded the trade results. The performance record was essential to validate a reasonable reward/risk ratio, win percentage and performance expectancy on a system.

If the performance record was not profitable, I would resume my system search. Until I had a system that was profitable at least based on its historical performance and predetermined evaluation criteria, I would not recommend starting the simulation.

Have to add that the traders must have a trading plan and daily game plan for the trading system and financial instrument before preparing the 100 signals. Please refer to the Trading Plan and Daily Game Plan chapters for guidance.

When I was satisfied with the historical performance and expectancy, I started trading in simulation. I stayed with 50 signals and did not have a completion timeline to safeguard over-trading and/or entered into a trade for the sake of meeting the quota.

On my daily game plan, I specified the maximum number of trades per day or week and no minimum number of trades. For whatever reason or reasons I did not place a trade for days (which actually happened), I would not feel the pressure and stress. In reality, stress did build up as I was not prepared for my reluctance to place a sim trade when all entry rules lined up.

It took me longer than expected to complete the 50-signal simulation assignment. I have to confess that no trade days caused substantial stress and a feeling of incompetence. If that happens to the readers, I will suggest a review and reflection session to find out what is the reason for the reluctance. In my case, it was more fear-related and a courage issue.

Once I completed my 50-signal sim assignment, I tabulated my trades to see if it met my expectation plus validating the result aligned with the historical one that I prepared earlier.

I had a Remarks section on my checklist so that I could document my emotion before, during and post trading. Going through the checklist helped me to assess my emotional state.

Additional Remarks on Performance Expectancy

- The less you lose = the more you will make!
- Consistency does not come easy!
- Consistency comes with practice and commitment!

Learn to be content with a system or else it could mean forever searching and testing! It is a very dangerous trap! It would mean a continued investment of time and resources with no timeline. It would be challenging to feel accomplished and likely to feel lost most of the time. Staying hopeful had kept me going for months. Only until I was willing to get settled with a system, I started developing more confidence and strength on the system and myself.

Are there rights or wrongs in one's trading journey? It is up to the traders to evaluate their progress. For me, I have no regrets in starting my trading journey and invested 8-10 years most people's working life in getting to where I am.

Being desperate had turned me blind literally and I made many non-sensible moves I mentioned in the book. The learning cost (mental pain and financial loss that I experienced) had made me a more informed investor. I am glad that I have an opportunity to share my learning with the readers.

SUPPORT AND RESISTANCE (S/R)

Traders talk about S/R all the time. Settled with or without an S/R indicator was an easy choice for me. Complicated indicators provided me with 10+ S/R levels. Simple ones consisted of two lines or previous high and low price indication.

When I was insecure, I wanted everything and anything on my charts. I went with a heavy-duty S/R indicator that would display 10+ S/R levels. Once I realized my scalping personality, I did not really need an S/R indicator as I was in and out of a trade within a 10-tick price movement.

Having said that, learned how to read price movement and became competent in labelling Higher High (HH), Higher Low (HL), Lower Low (LL) and Lower High (LH) was essential for my advancement to become a skilled trader.

I have been incorporating my S/R knowledge into my trade management. For example, when the price did not break up or down for minutes and was resistant at a certain price level, I often chose to exit when I was in a trade.

I also paid attention to responsive buying and initiative selling once price broke up or down. When I acquired the basics of price action, I understood the following logics:

The market opened with a big drop and no responsive buying. The price action indicated acceptance of the lower price and price would likely continue to fall. I could trade with the "initiative" activity (since no rejection and no responsive buyers) and place a short trade.

Trade with a naked chart (a chart consists of no indicators) could be intimidating. Spend some time to learn the basics will be beneficial if one is serious about Futures trading. I started very late with my price action learning. Once I overcame the initial resistance, I found it very beneficial.

TRADITIONAL/DISCRETIONARY OR AUTOMATED TRADING?

There are two camps for and against traditional/discretionary and automated trading. It is always the case in life and we have to make a sensible decision. Let me map out the pros and cons based on my experience.

Traditional/Discretionary Trading

Pros: I am the boss! Once I succeed in establishing a close bond with a trading system and a Futures market, I can trade at ease with my daily game rules all mapped out.

Cons: I am just human and will still be struggling with fear and greed on a regular basis.

Automated Trading

Pros: Set and Forget! After activating an automated trading strategy on a market with predetermined parameters (say trading time, contract size, profit target, stop loss and exit), I can stay away from the trade station. Minimal emotion issues pre, during and post-trading.

Cons: Unexpected technical and system issues when I am not at the trade station. Very often a bigger drawdown for running an automated trading strategy compared to traditional/discretionary trading.

Based on my experience, I believe one will need a bigger investment pool for automated trading. I have been suggesting a minimum trading account of US$3,000 with a discounted brokerage firm. For those who trade their Futures account with an automated trading strategy, I will recommend US$10,000 for each one-contract trade. For example, if I am going to trade two different financial instruments, I will need at least US$20,000 to trade them. I will also stay with one-contract trades until my account grows every US$5,000 before adjusting my one-contract trades to multiple ones. Please read How To Grow An Account chapter for a better idea.

Most argue that automated trading is the answer to minimize fear and greed from traditional/discretionary trading. Unless and until we are very comfortable with an automated trading system's performance, fear will always be there. Greed is manageable once we have a trading plan. The most challenging issues have always been triggered by the traders. For example,

- How do they manage their emotions?
- How do they manage their trades?
- Are they trading their predetermined trading plan?
- Are they following their daily game rules?
- Do they have pride and ego attached to a trade's performance?

Beth Fiedler

Comment: A trading system (whether it is a traditional/discretionary or an automated one) has to pass the suggested evaluation process. Please read the How To Validate A System's Performance and How to Tabulate Expectancy chapters.

HOW TO BECOME A CONSISTENTLY SUCCESSFUL TRADER?

Internalize these 5**C**s when running a trading business:

Courage
Confidence
Concentration
Choice-making
Consistency

I estimate that most of the above **C**s are self-explanatory except Choice-making. When a trading plan is process-oriented, we will be observing predetermined game rules to run our trading business. When our favorite signal in a trading system is process-oriented, we will be making choices based on a specified checklist of entry conditions.

Once we engage ourselves wholeheartedly in a process where the action is, we will stay in a Play zone where we feel relaxed and enjoy playing with options and be in the process.

It is time to make a pledge to the following:

Commitment #1: Focus and concentrate on learning one trading system at one time!

Commitment #2: Pause your indicator and system search when your system is overloaded!

Commitment #3: Stop making changes to your trading system!

Commitment #4: Pause when you have a potentially profitable trading system!

Commitment #5: Prepare a sensible trading plan and daily game plan (use for both sim- and live-trading)!

Commitment #6: Start sim-trading with a S.M.A.R.T. plan!

Commitment #7: Identify your favorite signal!

Commitment #8: Review and reflection on your own trading performance and your trading behavior!

Commitment #9: Stay on simulation until you have a proven profitable performance record to justify live-trading!

Commitment #10: K.I.S.S.

It is important to accept trading is a probability game. Those who can identify and play their edges will stand a better chance to win. It also goes without saying that those who spend time to take care of their physical well-being are the smart traders. There are always so many variables that tie closely with a trader's mental and physical fitness.

Start with the basics and always go back to the basics! Bear in mind that an indicator or a trading system is not going to make our trading business successful! It is always the trader who will make it or break it!

For most of us blowing up an account or losing thousands of dollars is inevitable. It is part of our learning. For me, the most challenging and difficult barrier had been to recognize my bad habits and unlearn them one by one. Having some trading threads to log my progress had helped me to review and improve myself continuously.

Trading skills and system/market knowledge can be learned at our own pace. Yet not more than 5% of the traders are successful on a consistent basis. Most traders have trading plans and only countable ones have been trading their plans diligently. Only a few traders are willing to put their pride and ego aside. We all want to be right all the time. We all want to be up there. Trading is a humble profession.

Successful traders are those who listen and want what a market wants! No one has control over the outcome of a trade or any trades. Until we accept this, we are not ready to trade live!

THE HOLY GRAIL

My recipe to create a holy grail!

Ingredients

- Acceptance of no holy grails out there
- BE in the learning and trading process
- A commitment to learn and become a disciplined trader
- Diligence in trading my trading plan and daily game plan
- Ease of mind and let go of pride

Development Methodology

- Review and Reflection on a consistent basis!
- Responsible for every move and trading decision!
- Repeatedly unlearn my bad habits (some have been persistent)!

Add tons of patience and perseverance - I have my own holy grail!

ACTION PLAN

MARKET REPLAY VS SIMULATION VS LIVE TRADING

When I started trying different trading systems, I often got excited with their performance results generated by strategy analysis. We all knew the results were misleading. However, I still consider strategy analysis a time saver to pre-screen a trading system before sim-trading it. My major selection criteria included profit factor (at least 1.5), average time per trade (must meet my scalping preference) and maximum drawdown (must be within my account size).

Then I would allocate time and resources for historical data, market replay and simulation. Once I reach a profitable performance competence close to 80%, I will consider live-trading the system.

Using historical data to validate a system's performance is preliminary yet quite effective and efficient. We do not need to wait for a live market.

Market replay can be used to serve as a learning or preliminary assessment tool. If the traders do not have time to sim-trade a market, they can still get some practice with market replay. Market replay is also useful for back testing. I knew some trading friends were doing the heavy-duty market replay for back testing purposes.

Beth Fiedler

Please commit yourself to a trading plan with predetermined daily game rules. Follow exactly your plan when performing market replay. Then apply a 30% discount on the market replay result.

Simulation is more reliable than market replay. However, it will not match live trading 100%. Having said that, simulation is essential to validate a trading system plus giving the traders some hands-on experience on a trading platform, trading system and market in real-time. Until the traders prove to be profitable on the simulator, do not "I repeat" do not trade live. Once we have a profitable sim performance record, cushion a 15% discount on the result so that we will be more prepared for a less profitable live performance.

Live trading performance could be very different from our simulation and market replay performances. It is because we will be trading our real money. I make an assumption here that most of us will be trading our own account and not trading as an agent for someone else. When we have real money at stake, the way we manage our trades and our behavior will be quite different from simulation and market replay.

Simple examples will be: our heart will likely run faster, our hands sweat more, and our stress level will be higher. Our tendency to hang on to a losing trade will be stronger. Plus, we will forget our trading rules, whether we are on a winning or losing trade. Greed and fear will be more dominant when we are in a live trade.

I considered myself a very disciplined person. Yet trading had turned me into a non-disciplined monster. I experienced behavioral changes when I was in a live trade. When my pride and ego was at stake, I could be disoriented and out of control.

When we live-trade, having a pair of predetermined profit target and stop loss orders are the key to protect our investment capital. Before entering into a trade (market replay, simulator or live trading), we must know our position. If we do not, we are not suitable to make any type of investment.

Again, no live trading unless we have an investment capital. If we do not have an investment capital, we can be on a simulator and start saving.

It can be challenging because trading (even in a simulator) is addictive. Most cannot resist an urge to place a live trade and open a trading account. Discipline is what a trader needs to develop. If we cannot resist our trading urge, we will likely end up over-trading and losing most of the time!

MY FAVORITE TRADING SYSTEMS

I have a few favorite trading systems. Yes, more than one. They all share the following characteristics:

- Countable number of indicators
- Simple rules to follow
- Very easy to identify a trade signal
- Win rate of 70% or more
- Specific entry point with a pair of predetermined profit target and stop loss orders

It took me two years to realize simplicity is the key for a trading system. Before reaching this important milestone, I was consistently looking for new indicators and systems not to mention my charts were always loaded with indicators.

Whenever an indicator caught my attention, I would do research to better understand its logic and parameters. For a trend indicator, crossover indicates a change of trend. The crossover definition was not good enough for me. I wanted to know more about the lines, numbers and dots on the indicator. I spent hours reading over 165 pages of posts. Got two red eyes for days. Sound stupid I know. My trading life could be simpler and easier if I learned to let go sooner.

That is what this book is about. Share my learning so that readers can save time, pain and money. They do not need to spend thousands of hours after going through what I have covered here.

Note: When designing a trading system, we must understand our trading preference. For me, I am a scalper and prefer to be in and out of a trade within minutes. Scalping first gave me an illusion that my system had to be a very small interval chart. I stayed with 3- and 4-tick charts and found them too fast for me. I started trying slightly bigger interval charts and ended up with 5- and 9-range charts for my system. Be flexible and try a system on different interval settings. Plus a good understanding of the instrument/market we are going to trade inclusive of the components of the market development.

FAVORITE SIGNAL

We must have a trading system that is good enough to trade on a simulator before learning how to identify our favorite signal. When I was busy shopping for indicators and trading systems, I never had the patience and awareness of learning my favorite signal.

Having a tradable system with a 70% win rate, I was under the illusion that everything would be very straightforward from that point forward. Unfortunately, my learning and system search did not stop there. There were and always are ambiguous gray areas of a trading system until we spent hundreds of hours of screen time on a particular market and learned the setup inside and out.

Once we created a bond with both the system and market, we would be in good position to outline the entry conditions of our favorite signal. I have been calling my favorite signal Triple-A and next to it almost Triple-A. Since I have seen the Triple-A signals materializing in front of me hundreds of times, I could anticipate its formation. I became selective when I got more experienced and comfortable with my favorite signal. I have more faith and confidence in the Triple-A ones and quite often choose to give the second best ones a pass.

I shared my insight with most trading friends who are still in search of a trading system. I believe staying with a tradable system long enough will build our confidence in the system. Our own trading performance will also get better over time. Focus on high probability signals which we name our favorite represents ownership of our trading performance.

It is a good idea to prepare a checklist on our favorite signal. For example,

First, both moving averages are rising or falling at the same time.

Second, there are maximum four ticks between the two moving averages.

Third, price must break above or below the two moving averages.

Fourth,

Fifth,

.. ..

To internalize my favorite signal, I manually checked off each entry requirement when I was anticipating its formation. This process has helped my concentration on the price movement and minimized unnecessary disruption or emotional issues.

I also used a video recording application to capture the signal development inclusive of my audio narration for about two weeks. I recorded my pre-, during and post-trading state of being in the clips. These video clips were extremely beneficial to my Futures learning. Not only did they re-affirm my understanding of the trading system, they also served as an emotional release therapy.

In short, I highly recommend taking steps to learn and uncover your favorite signal (maximum two and stay with one would be great). It will definitely help keep us on track!

Confession: I used to take signals that I knew I should not be taking. My conscious mind did its best to rationalize and justify my stupid decision every time. Almost all of these trades went against me immediately upon entry. I froze and failed to close them to minimize my loss. If we have confidence and competence to anticipate and execute our favorite signal, we will break the vicious over-trading mold.

STRATEGY ANALYZER

I only used one trading platform's strategy analyzer to get a better idea on some trading systems' performance. I estimate that most trading platforms have this feature. If we have an automated strategy of a trading system, the strategy analyzer will come in handy to provide us with additional insight such as Profit Factor, Maximum Drawdown, Average Time In Market, Average Maximum Adverse Excursion and Average Maximum Favorable Excursion. In addition to a comprehensive summary, strategy analyzer also comes with miscellaneous tabs. I often went through the Trades and Graphs tabs.

How did I start developing automated strategies? It was another unexpected incident. A trading friend showed me the data fields on a chart. I got an idea on how to make use of the data fields for the conditions and actions for a strategy.

I did day-and-night research and read many sample strategies available in different community forums. My trading platform partner NinjaTrader has a support forum. I created two trading threads there on automation. Whenever I encountered any strategy development issues, I would post my questions there. Very often within minutes, a NinjaTrader support team member would respond. Since the support forum is open to the public, I sometimes got constructive feedback from other experienced traders too.

If the readers are interested in exploring automation, there are sample strategies readily available. Most of them are not script-protected and the readers can familiarize themselves with the codes. Most trading platforms have built-in strategy wizards. Start developing simple strategies or make use of the sample ones.

I consider automation a fast track to validate a trading system's performance and identify areas for improvement. It is very important to note that most performance results generated by a strategy analyzer could be misleading.

I spent a few months developing over 100 automated strategies. Most of them had very promising performance results and an impressive profit factor of 1.5 or higher. When I and my trading friends started sim-trading these trading systems on different instruments and time zones, we got unanimously poor performance results.

My learning: A trading system with a profit factor of at least 1.5 may worth further exploration. If its profit factor is less than 1.5, continue searching for another system.

We can also make use of optimization and fine-tune the input parameters of a strategy. Optimization is the process of testing a range of values through iterative backtests to determine the optimal input values over the historical test period based on the best result criterion. It is getting a little technical for me. I estimate that there are merits to optimization and worth mentioning it here.

Not many have the skills to develop automated strategies and most simply lose faith in strategy analysis. I agree with them. It is more effective and realistic to trade a system on simulation. Please go through the Market Replay vs Simulation vs Live Trading chapter.

TRADING PLAN

Motto: Trade my trading plan!

I allocated an investment capital (which I am prepared to lose 100%) to my Futures venture. I opened a Futures trading account with a discounted brokerage firm based on the following reasons:

- More affordable compared to a full-margin trading account
- No monthly account management fee (applicable to inactive accounts)
- Free real-time data feed
- Minimal customer service calls

When I was learning and sim-trading with minimal or no live trades, my Futures broker did not add any pressure to my full plate. I could learn and trade with a peaceful mind.

Enjoy glimpses of my plans for Futures trading:

Trading Plan #1 (within the first three months – very flexible and they were not carved in stone)

Investment Capital: US$3,000

Trading Time: 9:30-11:30 am Eastern Standard Time

Trading Instruments: 2

Beth Fiedler

No of Trading Systems: 2

No of Trading Charts: 8 (4 for each instrument)

Profit Target/Stop Loss: 6 / 10-15 (I did not have a pair of profit target and stop loss orders upon entry)

Trade Size: Mostly multiple-contract trades (I wanted to practice how to trade with a runner)

Maximum No of Trades/Day: Not Applicable (I over-traded most of the time)

Exit Plan: Not Applicable (I did not have an exit plan)

Trading Plan #2 (after six months in Futures learning – still flexible and I did not follow my plan 100%)

Investment Capital: US$3,000

Trading Time: 9:30-11:30 am Eastern Standard Time

Trading Instrument: 1

No of Trading Systems: 2

No of Trading Charts: 6

Profit Target/Stop Loss: 4-6 / 8-12 (I had a tendency to move my stop loss order)

Trade Size: Mostly 1-contract trades

Maximum No of Trades/Day: Not Applicable (I continued over-trading most of the time)

Exit Plan: Time-bound or warning (Started looking for an early exit if the price movement stalled / when a trade did not go anywhere after 5 minutes)

I incorporated the following strategic changes to my trading plan as time passed by:

- Maximum No of Trades/Day
- Daily Profit and Loss (from $ to ticks)
- Weekly Profit and Loss (from $ to ticks)

Having predetermined daily profit and loss targets helps me stop trading when one of them gets hit. Maximum number of trades have encouraged me to focus on high probability signals only. I have become more selective and focused. Without my knowing, my over-trading habit was cured.

I prepared reminders and posted them on my trade station. For example,

- No 1 Trading Goal: Preserve precious capital
- Sit on hands (SOH) when there is important news
- SOH when there is no high probability setup
- Do not over-trade
- No chasing
- Trade My Trading Plan (No Exception)
- Pay Attention to Support and Resistance Levels
- Early Exit with warnings
- FOMC day (typically show and choppy) = Take the day off

Before each trading session, I started listening to some trading hypnosis audio clips. I also practiced an emotional freedom technique to tame my emotion.

It is important to have a calm trading environment to minimize chances of unexpected disturbances. If our day starts off on the wrong foot and we do not feel like trading, take the day off. The markets are there for us and there are always profitable trade signals waiting. Missing one or a few is not the end of the world.

Beth Fiedler

Current Trading Plan (No change since June 2011)

Investment Capital: US$3,000

Trading Time: 8:30-11:00 am Eastern Standard Time

Trading Instrument: 1

No of Trading Systems: 1

No of Trading Charts: 2

Profit Target/Stop Loss: 10 / 6 (Use an advanced trade management (ATM) feature to automatically place a pair of predetermined profit target and stop loss orders upon entry)

Trade Size: 1-contract trades

Maximum No of Trades/Day: 3

Exit Plan: Predetermined profit target/stop loss orders upon entry

Daily Profit and Loss: 20 /10

Weekly Profit and Loss: 80 / 36

    Note: I have an overall trading plan listing the instruments I invested. For example, stocks and foreign currencies account for 40% of my investment portfolio. Since I have a small investment capital, I have been staying with 3-5 instruments. Their accumulated total is always within a comfort zone of 15% of the available capital. Please go through the FINANCIAL PLANNING section to better understand your finances.

DAILY GAME PLAN

When I was an inexperienced Futures trader, I found it very hard to take a full stop on a trade. When I was an aggressive Futures trader, I found it very hard to accept a losing trade and/or being wrong most of the time. Once I realized survival was the key, I have been observing my daily game plan diligently.

There are overlapping items between my trading plan and daily game plan. They serve to remind me to follow the rules and trade my plan. A daily game plan will pan out everything. For example,

Slogan: Follow the game rules and trade my plan!

Trading Time: 8:30-11:00 am Eastern Standard Time

Trading Instrument: 1

No of Trading Systems: 1

No of Trading Charts: 2

Profit Target/Stop Loss: 10 / 6 (the orders are entered automatically upon entry)

Trade Size: 1-contract trades only

Maximum No of Trades/Day: 3

Daily Profit and Loss: 20 / 10

Exit Plan: Either profit target or stop loss order gets hit. No early exit.

To-Do List

- Trade my favorite signal only (no second best ones)
- Mentally check off all the entry conditions on my favorite signal's checklist before every trade entry
- Leave my trade station after a trade entry (I did that initially so that I would not be tempted to adjust my profit target and stop loss orders.)
- SOH 15 minutes before and after an important news
- SOH during 12:00-1:00 pm Eastern Standard Time lunch break (only applicable if I trade in the afternoon)
- Record my trade(s) on my trade journal (I included pre, during and post-trade comments. My trade journal has been an extremely useful tool for my progress.)
- Work on one bad habit at a time (I was working on chasing, over-trading and moving my stop loss order (just to name a few) until I stayed focused as a disciplined mechanical trader.)

Once we settle with a trading system which we name our own (could be simple or sophisticated), we will not be processing too much information. That's why I had a Favorite Signal chapter to emphasize the importance of having our favorite signal.

It is also more important to follow the daily game rules than having a profitable trade. Trust me! Do not be misled by an occasional derailed trade success. A profitable trade (which does not match our favorite signal's checklist) is damaging to our discipline development.

At the beginning, my daily game plans were lengthy and clumsy because I wanted to cover everything. As time passed by, it was getting simpler and skinnier. Yours too!

S.M.A.R.T. - REALITY CHECK

When I had a full-time job, I did not pay much attention to my investment portfolio. As I shared in the My Experience In Advisory Services chapter, my former advisors seldom asked the subscribers (including myself) to place stop loss orders on our investment (applied to stocks and directional options). When I was on an on-line option spreads program, they did suggest cutting loss at 3:1, ie exit when an accumulated loss was three times an upfront profit. However, in reality, the mentors often asked us to hold on to a losing option spread trade or even add an additional contract. In most cases, we ended up losing 50% or more.

Should we be putting a blame on these advisory vendors? When I was an inexperienced trader and did not know the importance of discipline and responsibility, I was doing exactly that. Having become a more disciplined trader, I have only myself to blame for my trading mistakes and success.

The biggest crime I ever committed was I did not perform a S.M.A.R.T. check on my investment portfolio until it was too late. A fresh new start gave me a chance to start all over with a petite investment capital. It is better to be late than never. I have become a more sensible investor who assumes a 100% responsibility for my investment performance.

For the readers who are investing or planning to invest, please go through the FINANCIAL PLANNING section. Should I have some guidance on the chapters that I covered, I could have saved over US$100,000.

What is S.M.A.R.T.? I have been using it for my personal and professional performance. The same acronym came in handy to measure the effectiveness of my trading plan, daily game plan, system and personal performance.

- **S**pecific (6Ws)
- **M**easurable (Quantifiable)
- **A**chievable (Reasonable expectation on both system and personal performance)
- **R**easonable (Realistic goals)
- **T**ime Bound (Time schedule with milestones and projection)

I did S.M.A.R.T. check on my personal performance more often than doing it on my systems and indicators. Knowing myself better put me on a faster track to address issues that I never thought were important. For example,

Investment Capital

Must open an adequately capitalized trading account. An under-capitalized one will never work. The #1 trading goal is and always will be to preserve precious capital.

Know Myself

What is my trading preference? When, where and how do I perform the best?

Trade Execution

Took me some time to build up the required courage and consistency in daily trade execution.

Risk Assessment

It is an ongoing process.

Trade Journal

Review and reflection! Incorporate any changes that will make my learning a more fruitful one.

Last but not least, practice makes perfect. I was quite rusty at the beginning and got better as I became more experienced.

REVIEW AND REFLECTION (R&R)

It is essential to spend some time taking stock of what are working and what are not. Pause and re-group may seem time-consuming. Yet R&Rs have been priceless in my personal and professional development.

I did not have R&R in my Futures journey until I got exhausted with my never-ending system and indicator search. Once I had my first R&R, I realized its benefits to my learning and self-development.

To get you thinking, the following list will come in handy (not an exhaustive list):

- Where do I want to go?
- How am I going to get there?
- What is my timeline?
- Am I successful?
- What have I been using to measure my progress? Are they effective?
- What is my ultimate goal?
- Have I been doing things that will help reaching my ultimate goal?
- Is my goal realistic and achievable? (Unrealistic goals are set. Then failed at or broken. It will be extremely detrimental to our psyche.)

- Do I have a trading plan?
- Do I have a daily game plan?
- Do I respect my trading plan and daily game plan? If no, why have I broken them?
- Am I satisfied with my trading plan? Regardless of a yes or no answer, outline what you have been doing that makes you feel satisfied or unsatisfied.
- Do I have an investment capital that I am prepared to lose 100%? If no, have I started saving for an investment capital? (Bear in mind that an under-capitalized trading account will have a negative impact on the trader.)
- Are my indicators lagging substantially when I compare them with real-time price movement?
- Are some of the indicators behaving (fall or rise) at the same time and same areas? If yes, review them and choose which one to keep.
- Am I taking counter-trend signals? If yes, how successful are they?
- Do I prefer signals align with the trend? If yes, are they more successful and represent less risk exposure?
- Did I stay in a losing trade too long?
- Did I keep moving my stop loss order?
- Did I let my stop loss order get hit even there was a warning for an early exit?
- Should I consider an early exit when there is a warning?

To prepare an action plan and track my progress, 6Ws have always been my best friend, ie

Who

When

What

Where

Why

ho**W**

Beth Fiedler

Enjoy a glimpse of one of my R&R extracts as follows:

1. Trading Plan (Done)
2. Daily Game Plan (Done)
3. Trading Discipline and Emotion State (In progress)
4. Trading System (Incomplete) (Market Profile (Fade The Extremes) was my primary trading system. I was trying to expand the setup.)
5. Trading Instrument(s) and Method (80% Complete)
    a) Instrument: Maximum two as a start (choices of ES, YM, 6E and CL). I will probably go with only one when trading live. Do not mind trying out more during exploration.
    b) Method: Discretionary or Automation or Both. I will be back to Discretionary while continue sim-trading a few automated strategies. I realize a big difference in my emotion this week, ie more calm and confident even I was sim-trading. Manual trading is not as intimating as before. Again, no way to tell until I am doing live trades.

Unquote

Take a few steps back every now and then. Evaluate your progress in an objective manner. Decide what are really working and what are not. Assess how you have been spending your time. Do you enjoy what you are doing and feel fulfilled? Pay attention to your mental and physical health.

Remember Futures trading can be either discretionary or automated. Do you want to be an auto trader, ie running an automated trading strategy to place trades? Or may be turned yourself into a mechanical trader (like me)? Mechanical traders are traders who follow their rules and trade their plan like a robot.

Remark: If R&R has pointed out that Futures trading is not for us, quitting is a sensible trading decision!

HOW TO VALIDATE A SYSTEM'S PERFORMANCE?

We have different methods and approaches to validate a system's performance. I highly recommend using historical data to validate a system's performance first. This can be accomplished by manually going through some historical data or using a strategy analyzer if we have a corresponding automated strategy for a trading system.

If we are satisfied with a system's historical performance, we can start sim-trading it in a live market. The key is to familiarize ourselves with a real-time trading environment. Before starting the assessment process, we must have a trading plan and daily game plan in place. Please go through these two important chapters under the ACTION PLAN section.

Once we are on simulation, we will need at least 100 sim trades to prepare a performance record. If our sim-trade performance on a particular system is at least 70-75% profitable, we may consider live-trading it. Our live decision will be based on our comfort level in executing our trading plan and daily game plan when trading our live trading account.

Go through our trading plan and daily game plan and make any appropriate adjustments. For example, halve the number of trades for the first week. Give ourselves a "timed out" when we have two consecutive losing trades in a row. The intention here is to give ourselves pauses when our live trading does not go according to our plan.

Review and reflection should also be a routine for experienced traders. Our trading plan can include alerts and warnings for pauses and trade halt like the ones implemented by the Exchanges. If something does not look or feel right, stop.

When we are on simulation, be sure to document everything, especially our thought and behavior. Successful sim-trading does not guarantee continued profitability of live-trading. Be prepared for surprises after the switch-over. I found it very useful to take stock of what worked and what not throughout the learning and trading stages.

For those who succeed in sim-trading as if they are trading live, they will stand a better chance to achieve a closely matched performance when going live.

Warning: Not many traders can really simulate as if they are trading live.

For most of us who switch from simulation to live-trading, it could mean a new start all over again. It is very normal and given time and patience, we still stand a chance to make it work.

If live-trading poses too much huddle on our mental and physical health, it is time to pause and do a realistic evaluation. Remember quitting is a sensible trading decision. I must emphasize again here that nothing wrong with this decision. If we have to choose between trading and health, health should always come first.

Let me go through the evaluation process in more details. A system's Win % represents its performance, right?

System #1:   Win % 70

System #2:   Win % 50

If Win % can tell us about a system's performance, System #1 is more profitable than System #2. Unfortunately, it is not that simple. Let's bring in their Reward/Reward (R/R) ratios and do a quick comparison on 100 trades.

System #1

Profit Target/Stop Loss: 10 ticks / 5 ticks (R/R 2:1 and Win % 70)

70 Winners x 10 ticks = 700 ticks

30 Losers x 5 ticks = 150 ticks

Gross = 550 ticks

System #2

Profit Target/Stop Loss: 50 ticks / 5 ticks (R/R 10:1 and Win % 50)

50 Winners x 50 ticks = 2,500 ticks

50 Losers x 5 ticks = 250 ticks

Gross = 2,250 ticks

Note: R/R ratio = Profit Target : Stop Loss

System #1 10:5 = R/R 2:1

System #2 50:5 = R/R 10:1

This is a simple example to demonstrate the importance to address different parameters when validating a system's performance. Don't judge a book by its cover. To evaluate a system, don't be misled by its Win % or Reward/Risk ratio alone!

I hope my book will give the readers enough information to work with. Or at least it will trigger them to ask questions and spend time to find out the answers. Trading is like any other life items. When our head and heart are in it, we will do your best to find out everything before jumping in.

Beth Fiedler

This is what this book is about. Make you think. Make you work. Make you listen. At the end, you will make an informed and sensible move!

HOW TO TABULATE EXPECTANCY?

It will be more effective if we have at least 100 trades to prepare an expectancy record. The following will give the readers an idea:

Daily Game Plan

Instrument: 6E (US$12.50/tick)

Period: 9 May to 3 June 2011 (20 trading mornings)

Time: 8:00 to 10:30 am Eastern Standard Time

Maximum No of Trades/Morning: 4 (1-contract trades only)

Trade Log

No of Trades: 78 (all 1-contract trades with signals aligned with the system checklist)

No of Winning Trades: 67 (Profit Target 10 ticks)

No of Losing Trades: 11 (Stop Loss 6 ticks / adjusted stop loss according to a Stop indicator)

Probability of Win: 86%

Probability of Loss: 14%

Commission Cost: US$417.30

Average Commission/Trade: US$5.35

Winning Trades Produced: 670 ticks / US$8,375.00

Losing Trades Produced: -29 ticks / -US$362.50

Average Winning Trade (after commission): US$119.65

Average Losing Trade (after commission): -US$38.30

Net Profit/Trade (after commission): US$97.37

Expectancy: (Win % 0.86*US$119.54) – (Loss % 0.14*US$38.30) = US$97.54

We will run this expectancy exercise on the historical, market replay and sim-performance trade logs. Let me show you how to benefit from the expectancy tabulation. For example,

System Expectancy on CL (US$10/tick): (Win % 0.75*US$82.50) – (Loss % 0.25*US$125.30) = US$30.55

If we find ways to lower the average loser by 3 ticks,

New System Expectancy would be (Win % 0.75*US$82.50) – (Loss % 0.25*US$95.30) = US$38.05

Compare US$30.55 with US$38.05, we will be making US$7.50 more per trade and it represents a 25% increase in profitability!

HOW TO GROW AN ACCOUNT?

Let me get it straight right from the beginning. Making a few thousand every day or most of the time is not realistic, especially if we are new to the Futures market and start with a small account!

The first time I received an email with a headline of making US$5,000/day in 10 minutes – my reaction was wild. How could that be possible? Then I found out the vendor used 50 contracts for a US$100 profitable trade. Most would not have the resources to place a 50-contract trade.

Please be smart and wise to interpret any products and services that may come our way. Do not lose our sensible judgement and be tempted into something we would regret later. I shared my mistakes in the book and hopefully the readers can safeguard most of them.

Please go through the To-Do List and Checklist chapters to confirm your readiness. We are talking about both mental and financial fitness to start a trading venture.

Most would recommend US$10,000 to fund a Futures trading account. If we feel comfortable to open an account with a discounted broker and are not trading on a full margin, an account of US$3,000 would be sufficient based on my experience.

Most inexperienced traders and learners will be sim-trading for some months. Some may consider a discounted broker who requires less than US$500 to open a Futures trading account. Be sure to go through the terms and conditions to safeguard any unexpected surprises. For example, a monthly account management fee on inactive accounts.

Some brokers charge a monthly management fee if the traders do not trade above the minimum number of trades. For me, I am cautious in spending money and quite often aim for cost and convenience.

I came across about 10 and tried over five brokers. I signed up with four for a live account at different timelines. There were pros and cons. Also depend on the instruments and markets we are going to trade.

For newcomers, I mentioned many times in this book that always start with sim-trading. We can sim-trade different financial instruments. For example, stocks, options, option spreads and Futures. I do not have lots of experience in FOREX trading. Only when I was experimenting with different trading platforms and systems, I placed some sim trades on different FOREX pairs or single FOREX instruments.

For micro-Futures, I only did a few sim-trades and cannot say much about it either. Micro-Futures could be an alternative for inexperienced traders because their unit prices are smaller. Some trading friends told me they did not sweat too much when trading some micro-Futures live. To gain more real live-trading experience (more on the emotion aspect), it may worth giving micro-Futures a try. Whether it is going to be regular or micro-Futures or FOREX, we must go through a simulation process before going live.

Also bear in mind that a trading system will behave differently on different markets. Different markets have different best trading times as well. If we consider allocating a predetermined amount and treat it as an education fund like signing up for a training program, it is doable.

Having said that, I still hold the opinion that we must sim-trade an instrument or market before trading live. Being successful in one market does not represent continued success or similar experience on another market. Trading the same instrument and the same trading system at a different time zone often generates a different trading result. It is very true. That's why I emphasize the importance of a trading plan with every tiny detail planned out.

For those who do not mind switching from one demo account to another after every 30 days, they can continue signing up for a trial account until they are ready to fund a live account and settle with a broker. I have trading friends who have over 10 email accounts. They kept switching their data-feed providers after every 30 days, ie when their demo account expired.

For me, I funded a discounted brokerage account (US$3,000) right at the beginning. I wanted to focus on learning and enjoyed a more stable trading environment. US$3,000 is quite affordable and it also offers me the flexibility to trade multiple-contract trades. For those who opt for a regular broker, I would suggest an account size of at least US$10,000 to accommodate the full margin requirement of one Futures contract.

If we have an intention to hold a Futures trade overnight, our account must always have the required full margin funding from day one. Some may argue that it is not a good move having any idling funds in a trading account. Unless and until we know our trading preference, stay with a demo account may be the best strategy.

Pairing with a broker who will meet our expectation (say customer support, commission rate and fee schedule, order fill, data feed streaming, trading platform layout and trade management) is an important decision. Before opening a live account, do research and sign-up for a free trial with a few shortlisted brokers.

We are all enthusiastic in growing our trading account. We must have a profitable sim-trade performance report on a trading system before preparing a projection table. Your sim-trade performance report will highlight the following:

- Financial Instrument (stay with one please)
- Trading Time (consistent trading time every day)
- Maximum No of Trades Per Week (to safeguard over-trading)
- Profit Target
- Stop Loss
- Win Rate
- Estimated Gain in Ticks/$ Per Week (I prefer Ticks and not $)
- Specific Accumulated Profit to Increase the Trade Size

Note: Start with one-contract trades. Go through the K.I.S.S. chapter again if necessary.

The following projection is based on all-in-all-out. I used the same profit target and stop loss for multiple-contract trades:

S.M.A.R.T. Plan (inclusive of daily game rules – collected data were based on sim-trade performance in a real-time trading environment)

Instrument: 6E (US$12.50/tick)

Trading Time: 8:00 to 10:00 am Eastern Standard Time

Maximum No of Trades/Week: 5 (started with 1-contract trades)

Profit Target: 10 ticks

Stop Loss: 6 ticks

Win %: 60%

Estimated Weekly Gain: 16 ticks / US$200

Accumulated Profit: US$2,000 to add one contract

Initial Account Size: US$3,000

Within a one-year time frame, one can grow a small account of US$3,000 to over US$40,000. I posted a short video on my website going through the whole projection exercise. You will enjoy free access after sign-up.

We must have valid data for the above parameters to tabulate a projection table. Bear in mind that projection is based on historical data, market replay and/or sim-trade performance results. For me, I did all three and not just one. This exercise was to illustrate that most do not need to trade big in order to grow an account. Trading is about consistency!

When we start live-trading a system, our live performance could be substantially different from the historical data, market replay and/or sim-trade performance results. When we have a S.M.A.R.T. trading plan with specific daily game rules, we will be protected from serious financial damages. What I meant by serious financial damages is we would only lose what we can afford and are willing to lose. Please go through the FINANCIAL PLANNING chapter to reaffirm your understanding.

ON YOUR MARK, GET SET, BEFORE GO

I was excited when I had my live-trading plan in place. I was not aware of the following checklist and was very grateful for a trading friend's sharing:

- No wireless keyboard! The keyboard must be hardwired to a trading computer.
- No wireless mouse! The mouse must be hardwired to a trading computer.
- Trading computer, monitor and Internet facilities must be connected to an electrical network with a battery backup unit. The backup unit must be strong enough to stay connected for at least 15 minutes after an unexpected power failure.
- Phone numbers of the Futures brokerage firm and their trade support desk.
- Pen and paper to write down any open trade information. For example, Futures name, contract size, entry price, position (Long or Short).
- A functional non-cordless phone with Item 4 numbers programmed under speed dial (if the phone is programmable).
- Ready to close an open trade by pressing Market or Flat or Close button!

THE WINNING STRATEGY

WANT WHAT THE MARKET WANTS

Who are the major players in a market? Unless we have the resources to move a market, most of us are retail traders who have no impact on a market. The only exception could be during lunch break when the major players are at lunch. That's why I emphasize the importance of selecting a trading time zone with enough volatility and volume.

Always pay attention to the Bid/Ask and volume. If they are not ideal, taking a break or closing down is a sensible trading decision. No trading is a trading decision on its own.

I came across some traders who stay close to their trade station for hours (say from 3:00 am to 10:00 pm) because they have nothing else to do. It is sad because I truly believe there must be other things one can do.

There are traders who trade with 5-10 monitors or more. I did before with four monitors. For the majority I would say 2-3 is good enough. I have no clue how effective one can be if he/she is trading 5-10 monitors on multiple markets concurrently. I shared my experience and it did not work out for me. At the end, I settled with two monitors.

Before entering into a trade, we must know where to enter and when to exit. If we do not have a plan, we are not ready to trade.

Beth Fiedler

Most trading systems are based on price action or market movement. Some markets move the same way with time lapse. Some markets move the opposite direction. For example, currency pairs like 6E (Euro Futures) and DX (US$ Futures) move opposite against each other.

When a trade was not working, the biggest mistake I made was to continue adjusting a stop loss order (when I had one) or did not have an order to close the trade. It was extremely detrimental to my account.

We trade according to price action and a market will not do what we want. The least we can do is to establish a safe trading environment for ourselves. Having a pair of predetermined profit target and stop loss orders based on our trading system is a must-have. This measure will definitely help minimize stress and unexpected loss that will jeopardize our account.

We all want most of our trades will work out and be profitable. When we figure out the profitability rate of our system, we are getting ourselves ready and more receptive to the occasional losing trades or losing days or losing weeks.

A losing trade is no fault to the trader or the system or the market. Traders need to know their system so well that they would not blame it for any losing trades. More important, they are not going to blame themselves for a losing trade or losing day or losing week. They need to take ownership yet do not hold themselves responsible for a trade.

I know it is confusing. We are responsible for our trading yet we do not hold ourselves personally responsible for a system's performance.

Let me elaborate more. We are the one doing all the research and hard work in testing and locating a trading system that we feel comfortable to trade with. We are the one gathering all the missing puzzles in good order and ready to go live after completing a profitable sim-performance assignment.

We are closer to making a decision whether we want to trade a system with our live account. If no, we will continue searching. If yes, we must follow what we have been doing when we were on simulation. There will be differences because we are trading a live account. It is very likely that we will manage our live trades differently. We will adjust our trading behavior to the best of our knowledge. We will follow the predetermined trading plan and daily game plan.

If we notice our trade management and behavior differ substantially (even we are profitable), it is time to pause and review whether the changes should be captured on a revised trading plan and daily game plan. The key here is to document our trading discipline and behavior on paper so that we always have a log to review our performance. Our log will safeguard a potential derail which may lead to a complete disaster.

Without discipline and rules, one can easily get off to a wrong track and develops some bad trading habits that could be challenging to fix. This chapter is a metaphor to alert us the importance of having discipline and consistency in developing a part- or full-time trading business.

It serves to remind us to observe what the market wants and not what the trader wants. Does our want matter? Unfortunately, the market (any markets) does not care about what we want. We must accept this reality!

Traders who have a predetermined trading plan and daily game plan would enjoy greater trading success and will be steps closer to become profitable on a consistent basis. Trading is about developing a routine with specific details. Trading is about owning a trading plan with a strong commitment to follow it diligently and consistently.

K.I.S.S.

Keep

It

Small and

Simple

K.I.S.S. is not amongst the mainstream asking us to aim high and shoot for the biggest/brightest star! To me, start with a small expectation on trading has been serving me better.

I went through a simple example in the How To Grow An Account chapter. When you prepare yours on paper and see the results right in front of you, you will be amazed. We do not need to trade hundreds of contracts to make trading a profitable experience for us.

Trading a big contract size represents higher risks if you ask me. Most do not have the resources to trade with volume. We are not aiming at short cash because it could easily turn into quick and substantial losses.

We need a peaceful mind to trade with minimal fear and greed. There are and will always be occasions when a trade runs well above a few hundred ticks and we only make 10 or 20 ticks. As long as the entry and exit match our trading plan, we should be happy to have a winning trade. Whether a trade ends way up or down after our exit does not bother or concern us.

Learn to let go and do not linger on a trade is extremely important for a disciplined trader. I would also like to point out that a single winning or losing trade should not have any impact on a trader. When we take a trade personally, we will run into an ego or pride issue which will cause unnecessary stress on our well-being.

WHEN NOT TO TRADE

This is a must-have chapter. For the first two years, over-trading had been a persistent problem in my trading career. I could not stop myself from placing a trade when there was no high probability setup based on my trading system. When I was in a losing trade, sometimes I could not stop myself from adding a second contract.

We all have our vices. Mine has been pride. My pride was an extremely important thing to me. I refused to have any connection with failure. When a trade was not working, I continued entering into more trades. It was an attempt to keep my pride around and I never wanted to lose it.

Unfortunately, trading is not about being right most of the time. Pride has no place in trading as it will blind us and we cannot see a market or ourselves objectively. Over-trading was a side-effect of pride and it has become an addictive behavior until I detached my performance from a trade result.

Other organic reasons not to place a trade include but not limited to the following:

- Narrow trading range
- 15 minutes before and after important news (safeguard being trapped)

- 15 minutes before and after a market opens (there are orders waiting to be filled at the open)
- Lunch break (lack of volume and volatility)
- 2:30-3:00 pm Eastern Standard Time (unexpected market movement right before the bond market closes at 3:00 pm Eastern Standard Time)

We do not need a reason not taking a signal (we may not be able to explain why – could be a gut feeling). Respect our feeling and wait for another signal. If we are not mentally or physically fit for trading, take the day off.

Do not force a trade when there are conflicting signals. This will happen if our system is a combination of multiple systems or our indicators conflict with each other. Do not force a trade when our trading time is almost over and we want to trade badly.

If we are trading crude oil Futures, we may even take the whole morning or a day off until the release of the weekly oil report. I had a real-life experience to share and it was an amazing reminder for me. I was sim-running some automated strategies on crude oil Futures and did not bother turning them off upon release of the weekly oil report. My stop loss order got hit and there was a 30-tick slippage when my exit order was filled. US$10/tick for crude oil Futures and that trade had incurred an additional US$300 damage because I was trading during the prime news time.

Imagine a trade does not have a predetermined exit and it is on live during the prime news time. A few thousand dollar account can be wiped out within seconds. I certainly hope that the readers will get this loud and clear. It is more important to identify when not to trade than when to trade!

QUITTING IS A TRADING DECISION

I have trading friends who have spent years and thousands of dollars on learning how and what to trade. Some have recently made a decision to focus on other non-trading issues and moved on without Futures trading in their lives. I respect their decision and actually no trading is a trading decision on its own.

Some chose to stay because they still believe they can make trading work for them. Having this chapter is important because I want to alert the readers that quitting is a trading decision. For some it could be a very sensible decision. After going through the whole book, I believe most of you will agree with me that trading is not for everyone.

We all have reasons to pursue certain interests and businesses at different timelines of our lives. I had a few mental and physical collapses during my trading pursuit. There were times I felt very depressed, discouraged and disappointed. I felt lost as to what to do next so that I could make trading work for me.

I was disappointed in my performance many times. When I said many I could have said most of the time. Until I got settled with what I had, I was in an ongoing struggle with hope and failure. Had greed been one of the emotions I encountered or had to tackle? In my case, not at all once I realized the importance of having a pair of profit target and stop loss orders before considering a trade.

Before learning how to be a disciplined trader and became one, I have to confess that greed was my biggest enemy especially when I had a full-time job. My investments in red did not bother me as much. I was making a decent living and did not count on my savings.

When I did not have a full-time income and was trading with scary money, it was a completely different story. What is scary money? My definition is money I cannot afford to lose. I did not have an investment capital and did not know how to tabulate one. Please go through the Understand My Finances chapter and tabulate your investment capital. If you do not have a reasonable amount (depend on the financial instruments and markets you are going to invest), please put trading aside and start saving instead.

Without an investment capital does not mean that you should stop learning how to invest. The good news is there are many trading forums and even vendors offer free learning opportunities. Just to make sure that you have the mentality and strength not to be pulled into high price-tagged programs and services that you cannot afford.

I would recommend cushioning a reasonable amount for learning. When I started my Futures venture, there were many complimentary services and products available. When I checked those complimentary resources again this year, over 50% were no longer available. Some have become more commercialized and asked for paid membership. It is understandable because they spent some years in recruiting free membership and it is time to get compensated for their expertise.

I have to add that when we started a system leasing business, the most popular question has always been "do you offer a free trial". Based on our experience, free membership has not been attracting serious learners.

For those who are not serious about learning and are not committed to giving it a fair try, please focus on something else. It is very important to have a strong commitment of both time and resources before starting a trading venture.

Some have a language barrier or computer operation issues. What should they do? Work them out first and be functional. For example, if traders are not functional in managing their trading platform, how could they manage a trading system and enter a trade when there is a high probability setup? There are basic techniques and talents that traders must have, both hard and soft skills. We all must be willing to face the reality and make a decision.

Bear in mind that there are many financial instruments and markets available. When you do your research, you will be in a good position to list them out and explore the interested ones one by one. List the pros and cons inclusive of their risk level and user-friendliness.

Some will not require a high degree of computer literacy. Some may only require a phone call with entry, exit and stop loss instructions. Before trading Futures, I often used an interactive service for trading stocks and directional options. Rarely did I need to give the service desk a call. It is comforting to know that a help desk is available.

When I was trading with scary money, my stress level was extremely high. Whether a trade started going to my favorite or against me, my heart raced at a record speed and my fingers started sweating instantly. These feelings never changed until I developed gadgets that turned me into a mechanical trader.

I also learned to detach myself (my pride) from a trade. Losing or winning now has minimal impact on me personally. There are ways to manage our emotions. I tried different emotional freedom techniques and hypnosis audios to release my tension. Taking breaks and exercises help as well. I will encourage you to explore different alternatives and practice some of them for better emotional control.

Bottom Line: Your physical and mental health should always be the priority and not making money!

CONTINUED LEARNING AND RESEARCH

We understand that there are no holy grails out there. Once we get settled with a trading system and financial instrument, we may think we can stay as-is for a long time.

Unfortunately, stability is not a norm in any financial markets. A tradable instrument could become a non-tradable one. When a Futures instrument moves in a very narrow range (say two to three points) for hours, its price action does not provide the traders with enough volatility to place a trade. When the same market behavior persists for weeks or months, most traders will start looking for alternatives.

That was exactly what happened to me when ES (E-Mini S&P Futures) became non-tradable in 2010. I started looking for alternatives such as TF (E-Mini Russell 2000 Futures) and 6E (Euro Futures). Remember a trading system may work for some, but not all. I went through what were listed under the ACTION PLAN section and started all over. Trading a different instrument justified the efforts made to validate a trading system before the switch-over to TF and 6E.

When our trade performance does not meet our expectation, pause for review and reflection. With accumulated trading experience and screen time, we will become more proficient in evaluating our trade performance and system performance. It is advisable to stay active in a few trading forums.

Continued learning and research should always be part of a business operation if the owners want to stay abreast of the latest development in an industry. Since trading is a business, traders will have their eyes and ears open all the time.

COMMON TRADING MISTAKES

I believe I made all the mistakes that traders can and will make. I repeatedly made the same mistakes over and over again for months before addressing them. Bear in mind that some mistakes kept coming back. Do not get discouraged!

I listed below my Top 10 trading mistakes and how to overcome them one by one:

- Unrealistic Goal
- Lack of Discipline
- Poor Trade Management
- Poor Money Management
- Ignorant Investor
- Traits of Non-disciplined Traders
- Never-ending Search of a Holy Grail
- Multicollinearity
- Use of Hindsight 20/20 Indicator
- Eagerness to Trade Live

Beth Fiedler

Unrealistic Goal

I was like most people who thought I could only win on every trade I was going to make. I was blown away when I was told that one can easily make thousands of dollars every day and only need to spend 15-30 minutes in front of a computer. I was naïve enough to believe that it was possible. I seldom paid attention to the fine print and disclaimer in the promotional materials. When I got more experienced, I started to ask questions about how the vendors tabulated their numbers. Most of the time, they used 50-100 contracts for one trade. It was totally unrealistic! I believe most would not have the resources to place a 50- to 100-contract trade on a daily basis.

The public has been fed with all these fancy and eye-catching headlines such as

- Secret to never losing a trade
- Allow you to automatically find guaranteed profit opportunities
- Low risk and without any hassle

No wonder most of us are under an illusion that we can only win! How to avoid this trading mistake? My suggestion is to develop a S.M.A.R.T. trading plan! A trading plan meeting these criteria:

- **S**pecific (Who, When, What, Where, Why and hoW)
- **M**easurable (Quantifiable Goals)
- **A**chievable (Reasonable Expectation on both system and personal performance)
- **R**easonable (Realistic Goals)
- **T**ime Bound (Time Schedule with Milestones and Projection)

It is also critical to observe predetermined daily game rules! I have included samples of my trading plan and daily game plan in this book.

Lack of Discipline

After going through my learning, I estimate that not many learners could be worse than me. These are the tips to stay focused and disciplined:

- Have a Plan and Trade Your Plan!
- Know Your Trading Plan inside Out!
- Must Have an Exit Plan for Every Single Trade!

For every trade (live or simulator or market replay), the trader must know exactly where to place a trade and will always include a pair of profit target and stop loss orders upon entry.

Poor Trade Management

I did regular review and recap of my trading performance. I prepared and updated my trading plan and game rules on a regular basis. They looked great on paper. When I was not committed to execute these plans wholeheartedly, I continued making the same trading mistakes and failed to protect my capital.

It took me over a year to understand the importance of identifying my favorite setup and became more focused. We talked about hundreds or even thousands of screen hours to train our eyes. I would like to add that our heart has to be on it so that we stand a better chance to create a closer bond with the market and instrument in question.

It is always very engaging when my favorite setup materializes in front of me. After internalizing my system and favorite signal, I became more competent in anticipating high probability signals that aligned with my system. For every trade entry, it has become a repeated action on my part to place a limit order (I seldom consider a market order) with a pair of profit target and stop loss orders. If my entry order did not get filled when price went off, I seldom chased. Instead, I cancelled my order and waited for another setup.

If there is only one single recommendation that I can give to my readers, it will be a 100% commitment to have a specific entry point with a pair of profit target and stop loss orders for every trade (applicable to both sim and live accounts). I know it is tempting to go wild without a boundary. Trust me, I was there. Trading is a humble business. Having predetermined rules plus a commitment to follow through is the most critical success factor!

Poor Money Management

I am good at numbers yet I failed hard on performing realistic and regular reviews on my former investment portfolio. It was an almost 100% write-off. The readers would get to know what happened in a separate chapter.

Capital protection is the Number 1 goal for money management! I have been applying this strategy to any instruments I consider investing. I created an e-Learning program "Are You Ready To Start Investing". My readers will enjoy free access after sign-up.

For Futures trading, I paid close attention to the following when assessing a trading system:

- What is the suggested profit target and stop loss?
- What is the Reward/Risk (R&R) ratio? (For me, my scalping system must have a 1:1 and ideally a higher R&R ratio.)
- What is the system's win rate? (For me, 60-70% will justify an initial trial.)
- What is the contract size? (I will only do 1-contract trades for a new system or an evening market. Be sure to tabulate performance expectancy based on 1-contract trades for at least 100 trades.)

Until my sim trade performance is 70-80% profitable, I may start cushioning occasional live trades. I will always have a specific amount that I am willing to risk on a daily and weekly basis. Once it gets hit, I stop trading.

I also have a predetermined investment amount that I would risk 100% on a Futures trading account. Once it hit my cutoff point, I would close the account. Luckily, I have not gone that direction after becoming more disciplined.

Ignorant Investor

I was definitely an ignorant investor until I started my self-learning journey. I did not have a good understanding of my finances. I did not know how to prepare a diversified trading portfolio based on my risk tolerance. Of course, I had no clue on how to tabulate a Trading Capital or an Investment Capital. I was not an informed investor in any aspects (both financially and psychologically). I did not have an exit plan for my investment.

Confession: I was not aware of the importance of an exit plan until I read a particular trading book. It is my favorite book and an eye-opening experience for me. Should I have read this book years ago, I could save thousands of dollars and heart pain!

Traits of Non-disciplined Traders

I only highlighted the most damaging ones as follows:

- Chasing
- Over-trade
- Too Aggressive
- Out of Control
- Unrealistic Expectation
- Don't Let Go
- Ego
- No Exit Plan

My weekly review and reflection helped to arouse my awareness of the above unacceptable traits. Once I realized how detrimental they were to my trading career, I started addressing them one by one. Yes, one by one and not on multiple traits. In my case, some of them were persistent. I was addicted to Chasing, Over-trade, Too Aggressive, Don't Let Go and Ego issues for a long time!

Do not get discouraged if one or some of them continue haunting you for a while. Persistence and perseverance got me there and they will do the same magic for you!

Never-ending Search of a Holy Grail

I was a great fan of a holy grail and had been on a never-ending search mission for over a year. I was actively looking for indicators and systems that would minimize my losing trades. I tried almost all indicators that I came across. I changed the indicators on my systems very often. I could be experimenting with over 10 new indicators within the same day. I removed and put them back on-and-off.

I signed up for multiple system trials for the same timeline. Quite often I had two to three trading systems up and running concurrently. I even had multiple trading platforms running (up to three). My trading fever hit its boiling point when I operated the following schedule:

Trading Time: 2:30-6:00 am | 7:30-11:30 am | 1:00-4:00 pm | 6:30-10:30 pm Eastern Standard Time

No of Trading Systems: Over 6

No of Instruments: Over 10 including most currency Futures

No of Charts: Over 20

No of Trading Platforms: 2

No of Monitors: 4

System conflicts were the norm. I minimized and maximized my systems and charts in a blink. I was weak on trade execution and did not catch one valid signal for weeks.

I was unable to find a holy grail because it did not exist and never will. To fill the gap, I expanded my coverage to the best of my capacity. Did it work? Of course not! I was burning both ends of my candle and experienced a stress attack.

It took me a while to recover both physically and mentally. However, I was grateful that I tried the above crazy schedule. It enlightened me that simplicity is the key. I finally accepted the reality that a holy grail did not and will never exist!

Multicollinearity

Multicollinearity was another crime that I committed unknowingly. What is multicollinearity? A simple definition: inadvertently use the same type of information more than once. A good example:

Use of multiple indicators all derived from the same series of closing prices to confirm each other.

Before noticing this crime, I have three or four indicators on my chart rose and fell at the same time and in the same areas. The simplest way to resolve multicollinearity problems is to reduce the number of indicators that belong to the same category.

Use of Hindsight 20/20 Indicator

I loved storytelling and no wonder I had a tendency to exercise the hindsight indicator very often to validate signals. Sadly, I must add – after the fact! I did housekeeping and removed COULDA, WOULDA and SHOULDA from my dictionary.

Eagerness to Trade Live

I traded live without spending hours on simulation and Futures learning. I was brave, right? Wrong, I was stupid! My eagerness was not restricted to Futures only. I was desperate to make money and placed live trades on different instruments (inclusive of stocks, directional options, option spreads and Futures) without learning the basics.

Honestly, I could not recall what happened. I could only say that my stupidity justified what happened to my trading account. I was the one solely responsible for the consequences.

Anyone who has the eagerness and enthusiasm to trade Futures, please commit to do the following homework before placing the first live trade:

- Hundreds of screen hours on each trading system (must be on the same instrument/market)
- At least 100 trades on simulation (signals that meet your entry rules) in a live trading environment (not market replay)
- At least 70% profitable sim-trade performance

Trade execution must align with a predetermined trading plan and adhere to the daily game rules which I covered in this book. The above captured the most important trading mistakes I had. It was not the complete list and hopefully would get the readers thinking about theirs.

FINANCIAL PLANNING

UNDERSTAND MY FINANCES

We must have a good understanding of our current financial situation before considering any investment. Let's find out what to do first.

With the help of a calculator, we will tabulate the following:

- Income (regular income which we get after taxes and deductions)
- Expenses (regular expenses such as food, accommodation and transportation)
- Assets (value of our possessions such as our house, our car, existing investments like stocks and bonds, and cash available)
- Liabilities (debt we owe, says mortgage on our home and credit card)

Once we tabulate these four items, we will know if we have a surplus or we call it available capital. If yes, we will choose a comfortable percentage on the available capital and come up with an investment capital – the funds that we may use to invest.

Investment Capital is the money we can afford to lose 100%. Most of us may ask "really 100%"? Yes! If we are not prepared to lose our investment capital 100%, trading is not for us.

Ask yourself honestly: What is the amount you feel comfortable to risk both financially and psychologically?

The norm percentage is between 3 and 5 on the available capital. There are traders who are willing to use up to 10 or more. Everyone is different and depend on the stage of life they are at. For the younger ones who will have more investment years, they may be receptive to a higher percentage. For those who are closer to retirement, they may choose a smaller percentage say 1-2 and not even 3.

Let's do a quick example on Investment Capital:

Income: US$5,000/month (after taxes and deduction)
Expenses: US$2,000/month
Assets: US$250,000
Liabilities: US$150,000

After going through the above Income, Expenses, Assets and Liabilities items, we feel comfortable to use US$100,000 as the available capital.

Available Capital: US$100,000
Investment Capital: US$3,000-$5,000-$10,000 (3%-5%-10%)
Risk Per Investment: US$50-$250 (based on 1-5%)

For conservative investors, they will consider US$3,000 (3%) or less. For more aggressive investors, they may consider US$10,000 or more. Another factor will be the brokerage partner. One can open a discounted brokerage account at US$1,000 or less. If we want to enjoy better commission rates on different financial instruments, we may need to open a trading account with a minimum balance of US$20,000 or more.

Now we have a big picture of our financial situation, especially our investment capital, we are ready to prepare a draft investment plan.

Note: I highly recommend a risk percentage on every investment (1-5% as illustrated in the above example).

PREPARE A DRAFT INVESTMENT PLAN

For a draft investment plan, we will allocate our investment capital to different financial instruments. For example,

- Stocks
- Bonds
- Commodities
- Currencies
- Derivatives
- Mutual Funds

As a newcomer, research on a few instruments and start with 3-5 would be reasonable. Focus on one would be good as well. Again, play safe and be cautious is always a great strategy for learners. Say I am interested in currencies. Currencies alone represent multiple instruments already. Am I going to trade in individual currencies? How about FOREX pairs? Or trading currency Futures? Or options? One market can easily branch out to many alternatives.

Once we have an idea of the instruments or markets we want to trade, we will prepare an investment portfolio. For example,

- Stocks 25%
- Bonds 25%
- GIC 10%
- Currencies 10%
- Options 10%
- Futures 10%
- Gold/Silver 10%

The instruments on an investment portfolio will always add up to 100%. Investors with a sizeable investment capital will have room to accommodate five or more instruments. For those with a smaller investment capital say up to US$10,000, one to three instruments will be within a comfort zone.

Whether we have a big or small portfolio, there is nothing to brag about or feel intimidated. Remember K.I.S.S.! Regardless of our portfolio size, we must allocate time and resources to manage our investments. If we are not prepared to perform regular tracking on our investment, trading may not work for us.

I remember stories about someone investing a few hundreds or thousands on an investment. Forgot about the investment for decades and it grew to hundred thousand. This could happen to a few and not the majority.

What is your investment strategy? Most advisors do not educate their customers the importance of an investment strategy, ie having an exit plan on every investment. If we are going to invest; it is not just about what; it is a must that we have entry and exit points. Also bear in mind that each market or instrument has its own personality. Time will help us develop a bond with the market of our choice. We will learn to interpret and understand their movement better.

MAKE A PLAN

We have at least a reason or reasons to make an investment. After placing a trade, the focus will be on managing it, especially before reaching a predetermined profit target. For me, trade management is about capital protection with an exit plan on every investment.

An Exit Plan

Directional Options – very often 50% is the exit point

It sounds big. It does. Unfortunately, for me 50% was not good enough. Most of my directional options trades ended up 100% write-off. What happened?

I did not have an exit plan. When my trade was making money, I did not realize a profit and held on. When it started losing money, I held on further hoping I would regain the lost ground. When the loss was over 50%, my urge to hold on was stronger than ever. When the loss was over 75%, I continued to linger in the hope that my trade would reverse and I could cut loss at 50%.

Almost all my directional options trades did not reverse to hit my 50% cutoff point. When the options dropped to pennies, they were simply not worth closing because the commission was more expensive. It was very sad and that's why I kept emphasizing an exit point must be in place upon entering into a trade. If not, please do not trade.

Option Spread – 1:3 Reward/Risk ratio

Traders make a profit upfront upon entering into an option spread. There are different approaches to determine an exit point. I recommend a 1:3 Reward/Risk ratio, which is a common practice.

When an option spread closes satisfactorily without getting any heat, the upfront profit will stay safe. When an option spread goes the opposite direction and hits a 3-time loss based on the profit made, it is time to exit. Did I follow this common practice? Occasionally and most of the time I did not. Why? It was again my ego/pride and my hope that the losing trades would reverse to my favorite. They seldom happened.

Trust me! It is better to lose 3 times the profit we make upfront than closing an option thread with a $1,000 loss. I had so many real trades with a Reward/Risk ratio of 1:10-20. I was my biggest enemy and held on to losing trades without a cutoff point. It was painful and a big lesson for me!

Note: An average upfront profit for an option spread has been US$50-75.

Stocks – a 5 to 15% exit

For conservative traders, 5% are big enough to cut their losses. For aggressive traders, they hold on to a losing trade up to 15%. Some stay between 5 and 15%. For me, until I learned the importance of an exit plan, I repeatedly made the same mistakes like other investments, I held on until almost nothing left.

Futures – 4 to 10 ticks for scalping trades

I have been a scalper at heart and do not stay in a trade after hours or days. There are traders who trade with a trending system that will allow them to stay in a trade for days or weeks or months. We need to find a system and instrument that will meet our trading preference.

Entering into an investment is easy. Everything looks good or for whatever reasons we decide to make an investment. Done deal. The focus then should be on the exit and very often we miss that. We all believe or hope that we will make money out of every investment. I cannot tell you how critical it is to have an exit plan, either for profit-taking or cutting loss.

Investment Expenses

In addition to commission and exchange fees, be prepared to spend money on any investment-related items. For example, books, newsletters, webinars, day trading room if you are day trading, paid advisory services and subscription. Remember we operate a business!

Advisory Services

I used advisory services on directional options, option spreads and stocks. They were not a happy experience as most of the vendors did not have an exit plan. When a trade was making money, they asked the subscribers, including myself to hold on. When the same trade reversed and we were losing money, they continued asking us to hold until it was almost a 100% write-off. Up to this moment, I still cannot figure out why!

You will ask me "Why I chose to hold on to a losing investment?" My one and only reason was "I hope that a losing trade would eventually turn around to my favorite." That's why you will notice I repeatedly mentioned in my book that if you are going to invest, you MUST always have a trading strategy inclusive of both entry and exit points. If not, I will highly recommend you to stay away from trading or investment of any kind!

If you are going to consider an investment advisor, prepare a Pros and Cons list on multiple service providers. I believe in choices and it is good to assess a few before making a decision. Here it comes a preliminary to-do list for your due diligence (you are welcome to add more items):

- What is the vendor's performance?
- How do you feel after talking or communicating with the vendor?
- Will you consider a trial or short-term service? (A longer term may be cheaper, but it will become more costly upon an early termination.)
- Does the vendor recommend an investment strategy inclusive of an entry and exit plan?
- How responsive is the vendor?

Time Schedule

We all have a busy life. Once we start investing, no matter how occupy we are (unless we do not care about our investment outcome), we must schedule some reflect and review sessions to track our investment performance. Each session will only take a few minutes if we log our investment on a regular basis. Once we have an organized system on our investment, we will get to enjoy our review and performance sessions.

KEEPING TRACK

These are the Keeping Track rules for every investor:

#1 Know what are you doing – ask yourself every time, why you decide to make that particular investment. Hopefully not because someone asks you to. If yes, that is not good enough.

#2 Be an informed investor

#3 Keep track of your portfolio

#4 Be prepared to exit. When it is time to cash in some gained profits or cut loss, no reluctance or hesitation to do so! An occasional losing investment is acceptable since there are no 100% holy grails out there. If someone approaches you and tells you it is a 100% win, please run! There are always risks and uncertainty in the financial market.

As a smaller retail investor (most of us are), we will not have access to an important news until the whole world knows about it. It is advisable to invest along with the major players. Trade with the mainstream. Very often the retail investors are the last ones to make money and they are the first ones to get hit. It is a reality check.

Investment is not a "Set and Forget" game! You are always responsible for every investment decision even an investment is based on someone's recommendation. Why?

- You are the one placing a trade!
- You are the one owning your trading account!
- You could have authorized an advisor to trade your account.

You are still the one signing off an authorization form.

Recap

Be sure you have these tools in place before and during trading:

- Use a planning tool
- Establish a timeline
- Stay with your plan
- Reflect and review
- Let go and move on

NO TRADING IF

#1 You are financially challenged!

#2 You are restless and undisciplined!

#3 You are irresponsible!

#4 You do not have time!

Investment is not about making a phone call to your brokers or place an on-line order! Having read my book, you know it is way more than that. If you do not have time to take care of your investment, do not invest. Or stay with only conservative investment items such as fixed term deposit and saving bonds.

It is important to know our limits or else trading will only bring us stress, anxiety, headache and heartburn.

INVESTMENT - FRAME OF MIND

I once thought I was smart and could predict price movement based on what I wanted. That smart thought became a big obstacle to my trading and learning. Ego and pride always got in my way as well.

After years of Futures experience, the following frame of mind will shorten one's learning curve:

- Mentality (Humble with no personal attachment and judgement)
- Discipline (Have a plan and follow the plan)
- Market (Establish a bond with a market and only trade according to the market movement)
- Reaction (Have a predetermined list of entry rules and react when a signal aligns)

To become a humble and sensible investor, it took me years to develop these traits and unlearn the bad ones. I have covered most of them in the Common Trading Mistakes chapter.

- Calm
- Competent
- Discipline
- Focus
- Responsible

I mentioned S.M.A.R.T. numerous times on my book. For those with an investment capital and are willing to give trading a try, be a S.M.A.R.T. Investor! Smart enough to make sensible decisions with a plan with these S.M.A.R.T. features:

- **S**pecific
- **M**easurable
- **A**chievable
- **R**ealistic
- **T**ime Bound

Putting on a trade is relatively easy. Knowing how and when to exit (plus having the discipline to do it) is what makes a trader a sensible and disciplined trader!

Bottom Line: Only Want What The Market Wants!

AN IMPORTANT MOVE

Ready to start? Let us do a quick check.

- Do you have an investment capital or will you start working on one?
- Are you prepared to lose 100% of your investment capital?
- Have you completed reading this book?
- Are you committed to accomplish the suggested to-do items on this book?

If you answer No to any of the above questions, work on them now. On a personal note, it will also be advisable to answer the following question:

- Do you see any obstacles (both tangible and intangible) that will disturb or interfere your learning?

If yes, address these expected obstacles before moving on. When you secure your own commitment to work on your learning, it is very important to document your progress in a written form. I highly recommend joining a community forum and create a thread. Or create a personal blog if you do not want to share your progress in a public forum.

Bear in mind that you own your thread or blog. It is up to you if you want to make it public or private. Others will definitely benefit from your sharing. Without your knowing, you will also start getting guidance from more experienced traders.

My active participation in different trading community forums has been the best and most effective learning tool for me. Of course it also depends on your commitment and participation in sharing your progress. You can continue to be a loner and do not really need to respond to others. However, if you are responsive and open, your learning will be triple-folded in return.

MAKE AN INFORMED DECISION

WHAT WOULD I DO DIFFERENTLY?

Now that I have spent close to 20,000 hours on my Futures venture, what would I do differently if I can start all over again? This chapter could be a blueprint for new comers.

Create a Learning Schedule

Allocate a predetermined number of hours per week on learning the basics and write a journal to capture the experience. Start with minimum two hours/week for the first four weeks. If the learners cannot devote two hours per week, it is telling me that commitment is not there and may as well put trading aside. Save them frustration and disappointment!

If the first four weeks go well and their passion is growing, adjust the number of hours to five hours per week. Then up to 10 (15 and 20 will be the next) if they are learning on a part-time basis.

Learning how to prioritize is always the key to success. Be realistic about the time they can afford without jeopardizing other important items and goals that they have in their lives.

If they have 24 hours per day at their disposal, a gradual adjustment up to 40-60 hours per week would be the ultimate. I am trying to map out an ideal situation here.

Beth Fiedler

Read and Do Research

Did I say before that the learners must love reading and doing research? If they are not, stop now and do something else. There are certain characteristics that potential traders or learners must possess.

Type in Futures learning on a search engine, they will be flooded with thousands of links. Nail down to one or two trading forums. They will be their homework for the first two weeks.

Browse a thread or threads that catch their attention. Start reading and get a feel for other traders' experience. They may even find a few free trading systems or indicators that they want to try.

Find a Trading Platform

Before trying a trading system or indicator, it is important to identify one or two trading platforms that the learners feel comfortable to use and trade on simulation. I tried about 10 different trading platforms. Very often users do not need to pay for a demo account.

Before committing to a particular trading platform, sign up for a demo account which usually lasts for a few weeks. Some basic ones could be free "forever" because they do not come with the advanced features. These basic platforms are functional and there are ways to get around trade management issues with more practice.

It is essential to gain some hands-on experience on a trading platform. Users must be confident to use it in simulation and possibly for live trading at a later date.

I ended up buying a lifetime license for two different trading platforms (US$100 and US$995 respectively). I have been using the advanced features for automation and indicator/strategy development. I also find them useful for trade execution. Remember my trade always has a pair of predetermined profit target and stop loss orders. It is an Advanced Trade Management (ATM) feature.

Open a Demo Trading Account/Find a Reliable Data Feed Provider

Complimentary data feed often comes with a demo trading account - at least for the first month. When I was learning, I moved from one demo provider to another for the first few months. Most of us want to complete our learning or evaluation process without accumulating an expensive bill. It is understandable and I was in the same boat.

Ask questions and we will get to know our preference. For example,

Trading Platform

- How user-friendly is the platform
- How responsive is the platform provider
- What training is available for new users
- What is the system license fee (subscription and/or a one-time purchase)
- What advanced trade management features or strategies it offers
- How legible are the platform layout and trade management section
- Is it a matured platform

Bottom Line: Learners' comfort level in using the platform to manage a trade (entry/exit)!

Demo Trading Account

- How responsive is the fill (find out the ping rate)
- What is the transaction fee
- What are the margin requirements
- Where will a pending order be stored
- Where will a pending order reside when there is a system failure
- Is there a help desk for off-line trade management

Beth Fiedler

Data Feed

- What is the time lapse on the charts
- How do the charts behave when there is an extreme fast price movement (test it on a fast instrument)

The above are not exhaustive and they serve to get the readers thinking. In short, we must feel confident and competent in using a platform to trade (inclusive of simulation before trading live). Sometimes we may not have all the preferred features on one platform. We simply make a sensible decision on the one that is closer to our ideal and adapt ourselves to it with more practice.

Trading is about making decision all the time. It is not on a single trade. It is more on what to do next and it is never-ending. I remember coming across a trading system that I really liked. Unfortunately, it only worked on a specific FOREX trading platform and I did not feel comfortable using that platform.

It haunted me for months. I spent lots of efforts in exploring different ways to convert the system and indicators to my preferred trading platform. I kept going back to that FOREX platform and forced myself to learn the operation. When every attempt failed, I stopped. Imagine the time I could have saved if I accepted the reality gracefully and moved on.

It is a good reminder that if there is at least one thing that the learners do not like (with or without a reason), please do not stress out unnecessarily and go with the guy's feeling.

Why am I saying that? An uneasy feeling (no matter how big or small) can easily affect the way we manage our trades. We will do ourselves a big favor to let go.

Remember to let go will free us of any emotional attachments we may have on a trade! For every trade, we will be making multiple decisions from entry to exit. Let me map out a normal trading process as follows (a linear view):

Identify a high probability trade signal -> Enter at a specified price -> Order gets filled -> Activate a pair of profit target and stop loss orders -> Exit

Do not label every trade with a win or loss will have substantial benefits to our mental and physical health. Without adding our personal pride and ego to a trade can make or break our trading career.

The most challenging obstacle for my Futures venture had always been my pride and ego. It is difficult not to take it personally when I had a losing trade or a losing day. It took me months to learn how to detach myself from a failure trap. We will have our own way to do it. Good luck!

TO-DO LIST

Learning Phase (3-6 months)

First thing first – Have you completed an assessment of your finances? If no, please do it now before reading further!

Do you have an investment capital (at least US$3,000 if you are going to open a Futures trading account with a discounted broker)? If no, please start saving.

Are you prepared to lose your investment capital 100%? If yes, continue going through the To-Do list. If no, please do not trade a live account as you are not mentally suitable for trading-related stress and financial losses.

Do you have some education funds (at least US$200-500) for the trading resources (say books and webinars) you may need for your learning venture? If no, either start saving or be willing to spend more time on research for complimentary resources.

Do you have a S.M.A.R.T. action plan with 6Ws on how to attain your goal(s) on this Futures venture? If no, draft one now.

Are you prepared to schedule regular R&R sessions to evaluate your progress? If no, you are not ready to start your Futures learning.

Depend on your availability, 3-6 months would be a reasonable timeline to complete the first milestone of your learning. Be sure to have a more comprehensive R&R at the end of the Learning Phase.

Initial Exploration Phase (6-12 months)

Have you finalized a list of financial instruments or markets you are going to learn and sim-trade? If no, prepare one now. I would recommend maximum two at one time, though you can have more on your list.

Have you nailed down a trading platform you are going to use? If no, it is fine to continue trying different ones. Be sure to stay with ideally one (maximum two) when you start sim-trading.

What is your favorite trading system? If you do not have one, it is fine to continue experimenting with different systems. Be sure to stay with maximum two (ideally one) at one time.

Do you have a S.M.A.R.T. trading plan? If no, please prepare one.

Do you have a S.M.A.R.T. daily game plan? If no, please prepare one that aligns with your trading plan.

Have you scheduled regular R&R sessions to evaluate your progress? If no, prepare a regular schedule now.

Depend on the time and resources you devote on this phase, 6-12 months would be reasonable to complete this very important milestone. At the end, conduct an indepth R&R on your learning, development, and physical and mental health.

Beth Fiedler

Your Next Move

Upon completion of the Learning and Initial Exploration phases, ask yourself if you want to continue? If no, your Futures learning has come to a satisfactory ending and resume your former lifestyle. Congratulate yourself for doing a great job and make a sensible trading decision to stop.

If yes, take a closer look on your three S.M.A.R.T. plans, namely

1. Action plan
2. Trading plan
3. Daily game plan

and adjust them according to your progress and trading preference. You will start another exploration phase and evaluate your progress on a bi-weekly or monthly basis. It is an ongoing process until you settle with a trading system (inclusive of your favorite setup), a trading platform and a financial instrument. Then you will start a new phase.

Sim-Trading Phase (6-12 months)

You will focus on trading your plans (trading and daily game plans) and enhancing your trade implementation and execution skills. Please go through the ACTION PLAN and THE WINNING STRATEGY sections.

Once you have a profitable sim-trade performance record of at least 100 trades (conducted in a real-time trading environment), ask yourself if the Win % and expectancy meet your expectation? If no, continue sim-trading and focus on trade execution.

Bear in mind that live trading is not a pressing issue and there is no schedule to make live trades on your agenda!

Decision Time

After almost two years in Futures trading, do you enjoy what you have been doing? Is Futures trading for you? Are you prepared to continue? How is your mental and physical health? You will probably ask more questions.

Whether you decide to stay on or leave the Futures playground, it is a great trading decision. You should always be proud of yourself in spending both time and resources to try it out. Congratulations!

CHECKLIST

Commitment Check

Rank your commitment from 0 to 10 (low to high). 10 or else forget about Futures learning!

How much time are you willing to spend? Minimum 2 hours consistently per week in a 3-6 month time span. Or else do something else.

Rank your willingness and diligence to do research and reading from 0 to 10 (low to high). Again, 10 to get a head-start.

Rank your commitment from 0 to 10 to do what were shared in this book. Must be 10 again!

Must-Have Skills

- Correct learning attitude
- Functional language skill to learn
- Research and reading skills
- Attention to details
- Follow and trade a trading plan
- Follow and trade a daily game plan
- Know when not to trade and stay out of the market

- Remove Coulda Woulda Shoulda from your life dictionary
- Computer literacy to manage and run a trading system and trading platform

Sundry Items

*Try at least three (3) financial instruments

*Try at least five (5) trading systems (free or demo)

*Try at least three (3) trading platforms (free or demo)

*Try at least three (3) data feed providers (free or demo)

*Learn at least three (3) indicators from Momentum, Trend and Volume categories

Sign up at least three (3) demo accounts with different brokerage firms (both discounted and regular ones)

Subscribe to at least two (2) trading forums (free)

Subscribe to at least two (2) trading blogs (free)

Subscribe to at least three (3) newsletters on at least two (2) different financial instruments (free or trial)

*One at a time and not multiple instruments or systems or platforms concurrently. Remind yourself not to fall into a never-ending loop of system and indicator search.

Basics

In addition to the Sundry Items above, I highly recommend acquiring some fundamental knowledge on Market Profile, two to three breakout systems (for example, open range breakout) and how to read price action.

Beth Fiedler

Nice-To-Have Items

- Listen to a hypnosis audio clip before each trading session
- Practice an emotional freedom technique EFT on an as required basis
- Post vision cards and reminders (continue to maintain a clean and tidy trade station)

Planning/Logging

- Prepare a S.M.A.R.T. action plan
- Prepare a S.M.A.R.T. trading plan
- Prepare a S.M.A.R.T. daily game plan
- Write a trading journal on each and every trading session (pre-, during and post-trading)
- Write a learning journal (inclusive of R&R thought and insight)

Note: Feel free to modify your S.M.A.R.T. plans on a continued basis.

To-Do Items

Please go through the To-Do List chapter. If you have a good understanding of the process plus a strong commitment to give it a go, you are ready to officially kick-off your Futures learning!

Note: You may not have a favorite setup to start with. You will get to see them and become more competent in anticipating their formation over time. Be sure to prepare a checklist of your favorite setup's entry requirements (step-by-step with every tiny detail). Feel free to get rid of the paper checklist after internalizing the process.

Open your eyes to see!
Open your ears to hear!
Open your heart to learn!

Remark: The Checklist chapter applies to trading in simulated, market-replay and live trading environments. It will be a good start for inexperienced Futures learners. I am sure that they will create their own learning plan to meet their personal needs.

ALERT!

Learning how to trade was a roller coaster ride for me. I started with a smooth ride then unexpected inversions along the way with no end. That was how I felt until I had a better grasp on traders' secrets.

How I, as a rider, position on the roller coaster to experience a ride is critical. Where I position myself and the types of thrill elements that I experience at different points have made a ride an unforgettable life experience.

The inversions, such as vertical loops, that turn my world upside down can closely describe how I felt and experienced on a physical and mental basis when I was learning how to trade Futures. My roller coaster ride on Futures was an exciting one. I had absolutely no idea on what to expect. There were times my ride got so out of control that I felt collapsing. Did quitting ever come up? Of course and luckily it flashed and disappeared within seconds.

I felt defeated and cheated by the markets hundreds of times. I moved from one financial instrument to another. I focused on one market and moved to multiple markets and moved back to one. I traded one system and moved to multiple and back to one. All I wanted was to rectify my pride and confidence in myself. It was more a battle of emotions inside me. For example,

- Hope and Despair
- Fear and Greed
- Quitting and Staying
- Failure and Success

I reminded myself very often not to become skeptical in life. My Futures venture had provided me with a playground to fall many times. I learned how to struggle up and accepted failure without taking it too personally at the end. I believe I have become a better person during and after the journey.

Ride Sharing

Do our best to stay with a clear head and mind all the time. Desperation will turn us vulnerable and tempt us to make non-sensible decision. Pause when we feel lost and helpless. We must gather our thought and re-gain our balance before making any decision or make a move.

It will always be acceptable to take a step backward or stay where we are. Take our time to review and refresh what alternatives we have. Be aware of tempting offers (like a candy upfront) yet we will be lured to a black hole within days. Remember the attractive pitches almost all vendors will be overloading us every day. We must stay alert even when we are desperate!

My book is to provide a one-stop solution by addressing all of the factors critical to Futures learning. Trading and money management are important, yet I kept bringing up the importance of mental and physical health. Health should always be a priority item in life.

In addition, be aware of the following side-effects of trading:

- Trading may turn us skeptical and suspicious!
- We may become un-balanced!
- We may lose the purpose of life!
- We may become a trading addict and miss out all the other fun things in life!

With the exception of the first side-effect, I had the remaining ones and took me months to recover. I certainly hope that my experience would enlighten the readers not to commit the same crimes.

CALL FOR ACTION

I started my Futures learning in June 2009. I was lucky that I came across many complimentary resources offering me:

- Free access to trading forums
- Free membership to trading clubs
- Free trials to a few trading rooms
- Free subscription of newsletters and webinars
- Free access to trading systems, indicators and trading books

When I checked my complimentary resources this summer, over 50% of them have become obsolete, 25% now ask for a subscription fee, and only 25% stay free and active. Time is the currency for the 21st century. If we are going to learn a new skill or explore an opportunity, it is better to act soon. No more procrastination or it will get more expensive and time-consuming.

We have run a system leasing business since summer 2011. Hundreds have knocked at our door. Less than 10% have taken action. What does it tell us? Procrastination is in our blood. Until an issue becomes pressing, most of us will choose to wait. Is it wrong to wait? Guess not. For whatever reasons, the timing is not right, we just have to respect our decision.

Beth Fiedler

If Futures trading has been on your to-do list for months or years, start listing the pros and cons of starting your Futures learning. I did a similar exercise when I was reluctant to go live after sim-trading for months with an impressive performance record. Listing or saying out loud our concerns help addressing both tangible and intangible obstacles on our way.

Ask yourself what have you got to lose?

ENDING NOTE

LOSSES AND GAINS

My Losses

- Sleep
- Hundreds of thousands of hours
- Quality time with my husband, family and friends

My Gains

- Hundreds of trading friends from different parts of the world
- Tender, Love and Care (TLC) from my husband, family and best friends
- Courage, Patience and Perseverance
- Sharper senses and more informed investment decision
- More survival skills
- An exit plan for every investment
- Additional inches because I sat and watched the markets like a hawk almost 24/7 for months

After starting a self-learning Futures journey, I had not been losing a substantial amount of money on my Futures trades. I always have an exit plan (a pair of predetermined profit target and stop loss orders) before and upon a trade entry. I know my risk before each trade entry. I always know where my entry point is. If I do not get filled, I will cancel my order and wait for another high probability setup. I have the patience to wait for another trading session if my trading morning ends with no trade. I learn not to force a trade and have not been committing an over-trade crime for years.

I also learned how to

- Understand my finances
- Tabulate an investment capital
- Cushion different risk levels to my investment portfolio
- Commit to trade on simulation before trading live
- Prepare trade performance report
- Evaluate system performance
- Tabulate system expectancy
- Draft S.M.A.R.T. plans
- Create indicators and systems
- Develop automated trading strategies

plus becoming a disciplined investor are the gains that I treasure and will benefit for life.

I sincerely hope that the readers will enjoy and treasure their learning. Given time and commitment, they will realize substantial gains with minimal expenses.

CONCLUSION

Attitude matters! Let me get it straight right from the beginning. Trading is running a business. This applies to the learning stage as well. When we are on simulation, we are committed to the best of our knowledge and ability to sim-trade as if we are trading our live account. Those who are going to give Futures a try, they must have read the MAKE AN INFORMED DECISION section a few times.

I love baking. Let me use it to get my message across.

First, what are we baking?

Second, what are the main ingredients?

Third, what are the optional ingredients (if any)?

Fourth, what kind of oven and baking utensils do we use?

Fifth, how much do we need to make?

Sixth, how much time do we have before delivery?

Seventh, are we familiar with the oven and baking utensils?

Eighth, where can we get help (if required)?

It is easier to be a better cook than becoming a good baker. Why? To prepare a delicious meal, we do not need the exact recipes for the dishes. If something goes wrong, there are often remedial steps we can take to fix a dish.

Baking is a different story. For example, if an ingredient is missing and the bakery item is in an oven, nothing can be done during and after the baking process. Another example is if the baking method is below or above the correct temperature, the bakery item will end up under-cooked (too raw) or over-cooked (too dry). Both are not edible and no post-baking remedial action will be available to fix it.

Good Futures traders are disciplined traders who trade their trading plan to the dot. They are like good bakers who follow each and every great recipe with care and attention to details. For example, they understand time is critical. When they see their favorite signal, they will not be hesitant for one millisecond and place an order right on time. They can anticipate their favorite signal's formation and know exactly where to enter. They are flawless in their trade execution.

Disciplined traders know their system inside out. They understand simplicity is the key. They will not have indicators act at the same time and in the same areas. Just like bakers, they will not use excessive sugar or salt (or other condiments) on their recipes.

If traders are bakers, they all have a sweet tooth of different sweetness preference. My favorite cupcakes could be too bland for others. While others' favorite cupcakes could be too sweet for me. We may be using the same trading system, yet our trading results will often differ (which I explained in more details in the Same Trading System Generates Different Trading Results chapter).

Be a learning sponge and enjoy the learning process. It will be a fulfilling and fruitful experience that helps uncover your talents and vices.

Good Luck and Happy Learning!

MY VISION

I was with different financial service and product providers. Most ask for thousands of dollars for their trading systems and training programs. Some ask for hundreds of dollars for their trading room and system subscription. I have not come across one that will offer a comprehensive training package that covers:

- A live training room that is running when a market is open
- A trading system that is very easy to understand and learn
- Ongoing education webinars that will help learners to develop and become more disciplined traders
- A FAQ blog where questions will be posted
- A learning platform that will allow users to share and chat 24/7

I believe most learners would appreciate an affordable platform

- where they can ask questions and know they will always get an honest response
- where they can learn how and where to start
- where they can share and learn wherever and whenever they are
- where they have a moderator whom they can trust and learn from

Another dream project has always been an experiential training program on fear and greed. I would love to incorporate real-time Futures trading to a training program so that the learners can experience real-time emotional challenges with pressing time-sensitive decision-making.

I shared these two visionary projects with different investors and partners over the years. My husband teased me that I was barking at the wrong trees. Unfortunately, he is right so far. May be I will get connected with a visionary investor or an educator in the future.

BEFORE AND AFTER

Some of you may want to have glimpses of my BEFORE and AFTER trading systems.

BEFORE knowing the trading secrets, my trading systems were illegible and untradeable. My charts were extremely crowded with indicators and conflicting signals.

AFTER knowing the trading secrets, my trading system has two charts. They have been more legible and tradeable.

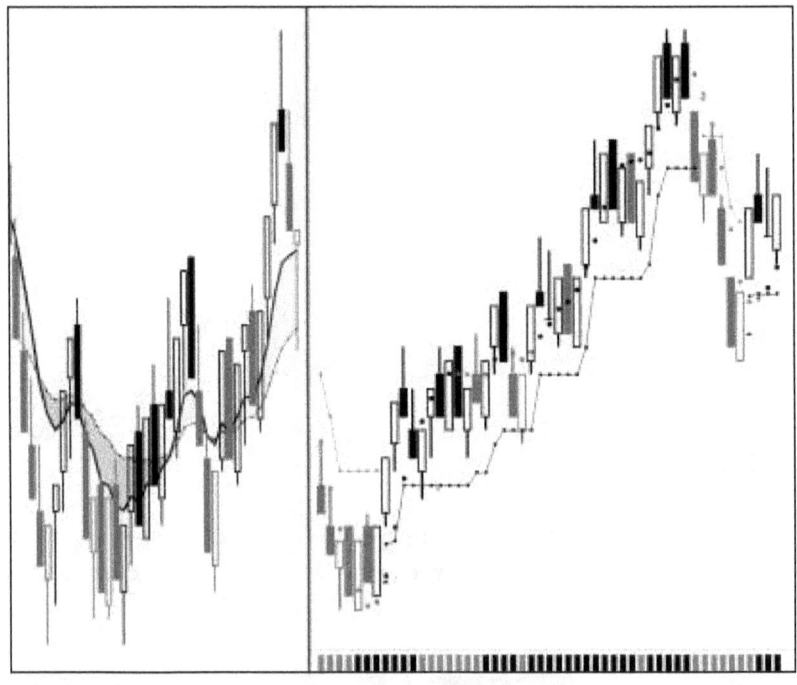

SIGN-UP

Those who sign up at www.bethfiedler.com will enjoy free access to the following e-Learning program:

- Are You Ready To Start Investing

I share my investment mistakes in this program. Some of its highlights were also in this book.

I also included a list of resource links for those who may want to start their learning in the very near future. Enjoy!

BONUS ARTICLES

Trading is not about luck. If luck is involved, I will not be anywhere close to trading. Why? Luck has never been in my life!

I have been counting on hard work, persistence and perseverance to achieve what I have accomplished. It was not a joke or an exaggeration that I worked almost 24/7 in 2009-2011. I was haunted by indicators and trading systems day and night. They were in my dreams and they were everywhere. Very often I woke up around 2:00 am in the morning and could not resist checking the London market. Originally meant to be a short glimpse and often ended up staying at my trade station for hours.

When I was developing my own indicators and automated trading strategies, I got stuck very often on codes and programming scripts. When there was an unresolved logic on my indicator or strategy, I could not stop working on it until the bug was fixed. I understand that I am not a techie and will never become one. However, I truly believe in persistence and perseverance.

Enclosed two bonus articles for those who want to know me better. Thank you!

My Roller Coaster Ride

Bio for A Non-profit Website

Everyone has a unique story. I am thrilled to share mine with you!

I was born in Hong Kong. My father was an electrician and owned a store. My mother was a full-time housewife taking care of four children. It was very unfortunate that my father passed away unexpectedly when I was six. You could imagine the challenges my mother faced as she was only 30 - a single mother of four (8-6-4-2).

Nothing fancy for my childhood and teenager lives. However, I did not miss anything because my mother took good care of me. I never worried about food and education. She always wanted one of us to have a university degree.

I worked very hard and strived to save some education funds. Canada was very receptive to professional immigrants back in the 80's. I applied to both Canada and Australia as an administrative professional. Got their visas within months.

I chose Canada because it struck me as a very open and diversified country. I also loved their education system. Very affordable at that time for one with a landed immigrant status.

My university life has always been the best time of my life. I completed all the required credits a year sooner than most fellow students. Why and how? I took 10 credits in Fall/Winter and max out the summer programs as well. A typical day:

Beth Fiedler

Got up at 6:00 am. Bought a small coffee and occasionally a bagel with cream cheese before an 8:00 am class. I often had half a bagel left for dinner around 8:00 pm when I worked as a lab monitor. To save some transportation money, I would choose to walk instead of spending a subway token. Winter times could be quite challenging. Back to the 90's we had severe winter days around -40 degree C with wind-chill. You may be curious to know how much I saved for not taking a subway train. It was less than a dollar.

There were months I considered Wonder Bread as my best friend. I had two slices as my daily meal. Occasionally with margarine when it was on sale for less than a dollar. Most would feel sorry for me as I did live like a church mouse for my university years.

I completed my university degree with honors and had always been one of the favorite students of most lecturers. Being alone in a foreign country, I had only myself to count on. If I had questions, my shaking hand would be the first one up to ask questions.

If you have a dream that's worth pursuing, go for it! Enjoy the tangible challenges and intangible rewards during the pursuit! Good luck!

Win Or Lose (A Contest Speech)

Do you recognize this person? Imagine her without her glasses and long hair. She was me, about 8 years ago. Hiding behind my glasses, hoping that no one would see me. My glasses gave me a false sense of security; funny, is it not?

A week before my 6 year old birthday, my father passed away suddenly. Overnight, I turned from a little princess to nobody. Like any other kids, I longed for my mother's attention and love. But compared to my sisters, brother, and all my peers, I was, to put it in my mother's words, "the ugly duckling". It made little difference whether I did well in my studies or not. I was still the shabby one, with teeny weenie eyes, a flat nose and a big mouth.

The more I craved for love and compliment, the more I was mocked. As I grew up, I began to withdraw from those around me. I seldom spoke or uttered a simple word, like yes or no. The best I did was nodding or shaking my head. No one ever seemed to notice I was suffering.

For over 15 years, I was haunted by one long bad dream. Night after night, I struggled endlessly to overcome an unknown force. Imagine yourself bound in your worst nightmare, unable to move an inch or speak a word. Feeling my helplessness, how was I going to break that spell?

In 1988, I emigrated to Toronto, and was lucky to have a tough-minded optimist as my boss. Walter shared with me his life experiences and gave me a lot of encouragement. His philosophy is "never sell yourself short and under-estimate your abilities". From Walter, I learned to observe everything around me differently and with appreciation.

Mother Nature was a great medicine to me. I spent hours watching and feeding seagulls, sitting on a staircase overlooking Lake Ontario, cycling along the lake shores, or playing hide-and-seek with my animal friends made me feel the whole world was in my hands. There is nothing ugly to the Mother Nature. Everything has its place and is beauty under the Sun.

Life is a precious gift and I promise myself to enjoy each passing moment. Who would accept me if I don't accept myself? I gradually released myself from my confined prison and was proud to be part of the Universe. Looking back, I started to realize my innocence for not understanding the hardship my mother went through. Preoccupied with the sudden loss of her husband and became a single parent of four small children, she had very little time to stop and see what was going deep down in her second daughter. Turning from ignorance, I admire my mother with all my heart. I told myself: it doesn't matter how many times I fall, as long as I have the courage to get up and start all over again.

We are responsible for ourselves. Destiny is not a matter of chance, it is a matter of choice. We pave our paths and paint our lives.

You can see now, I no longer hide behind my glasses, nor shut myself away from people. If someone sees me as a Cinderella or an ugly duckling, so be it. I will live the life of my choice and strive to reach my dream.

I challenge you all to listen to your heart and retrieve your long forgotten dream. Promise yourself this minute, you will make it. Take a chance, what have you got to lose?

LEGEND

FOMC = The Federal Open Market Committee

K.I.S.S. = Keep It Small and Simple

R&R = Review & Reflection

R/R Ratio = Reward/Risk Ratio

S.M.A.R.T. = Specific-Measurable-Achievable-Realistic-Time Bound

S/R = Support and Resistance

Sim-trading = Trading with a Simulator

SOH = Sit On Hands (No trading)

6E = Euro Futures

CL = Crude Oil Futures

DX = US$ Futures

ES = E-Mini S&P Futures

TF = E-Mini Russell 2000 Futures

YM = Dow Jones Futures

BIOGRAPHY

Beth is a dynamic lady with extensive life experience in both Eastern and Western environments. She has lived and worked in three international cities (Beijing, Hong Kong and Toronto) and travelled extensively across 15+ countries (over 100 cities).

She has gained substantial insight into different organizational cultures and management practices from her various management positions and consultation projects. For example,

- Founder
  EZ Color Trading
- General Manager
  Fleming International Limited, Hong Kong and Shenzhen
- Assistant Vice President, Operations Management
  AIG Finance (Hong Kong) Limited, Hong Kong
- Senior Credit Administrator
  Swiss Bank Corporation (Canada), Toronto
- Office Manager
  WJS International Inc, Beijing

Beth fell in love with training after years of Toastmasters learning. Her starting a consulting and soft skills training business (= leaving a senior management position with AIG) had surprised a lot of people.

Beth has touched thousands of lives on a global basis. She inspired hundreds of people to become a public speaking member. She was the owner and organizer of a multi-million HK$ Christmas function. Her threads have had close to 120,000 views as of summer 2013.

Her quality leadership and passion have attracted lots of media attention. Beth was interviewed by AlterMedic.com, Hamilton Spectator, Metro Broadcast Hong Kong, Toronto CBCC and The Record (a local newspaper of the Kitchener/Waterloo region in Ontario Canada). Stories about her vision were reported in The Record, Oriental Daily, Apple Daily, Hong Kong Economic Times, The Sun, Sing Tao Daily, Ming Pao, Central Magazine, Eat & Travel, and Sisters. Her most recent media appearances were on the CBC Dragons' Den (Toronto), Season VIII and Season IX.

Beth is known for her big heart in sharing. She has a strong passion of helping others excel!

Beth Fiedler

Professional Accomplishments

Area Governor of the Year, Toastmasters International, Pan-Southeast Asia Pacific Region

Distinguished Toastmaster (DTM), Toastmasters International, Hong Kong Division

Distinguished President's Area Award, Toastmasters International USA

Co-chair of the First District Toastmasters Convention in Hong Kong, Toastmasters International, Hong Kong Division

Champion of an Inter-club Evaluation Contest, Toastmasters International, Hong Kong

Designer/Facilitator of 150+ of Experiential Training Programs, Facilitation Sessions and Speaking Assignments (Canada, China PRC, Macau, Pan-Southeast Asia Pacific Region, Saudi Arabia, Taiwan ROC, The Philippines and USA)

Organizer/Advisor of 200+ Public and Private Functions (up to 7,000 participants) (Canada, China PRC, Macau, Pan-Southeast Asia Pacific Region, Taiwan ROC, Thailand, The Philippines and USA)

Academic Accomplishments

Bachelor of Applied Arts (Hons)
School of Administration and Information Management
Ryerson University, Toronto, Canada

Diploma in Adult Training and Development
University of Toronto, Toronto, Canada

Certified Social Media Strategist
Social Media Marketing University, USA

Certificates in Teaching English to Speakers of Other Languages
TESL, Ottawa, Canada
Trinity College London, England

Canadian Securities Course (Hons)
The Canadian Securities Institute, Toronto, Canada

Diploma in Multimedia Web Site Design
Unisoft Education Center, Hong Kong

http://www.ezcolortrading.com

http://www.wp-winpro.weebly.com

www.ingramcontent.com/pod-product-compliance
Lightning Source LLC
Chambersburg PA
CBHW070146100426
42743CB00013B/2826